The Surrendered Wife

A Woman's Spiritual Guide to
True Intimacy with a Man

Laura Doyle

Edited by Christine Gordon

St. Monday Publishing
Costa Mesa, CA

St. Monday books are available at special quantity discounts for bulk purchases for sales promotions, premiums, fund-raising and educational needs. Special books, or book excerpts can also be created to fit specific needs.

For details write St. Monday Publishing, 3051 Hayes Ave., Costa Mesa, CA 92626 or call 714/979-2152.

St. Monday Publishing
3051 Hayes Avenue
Costa Mesa, CA 92626

Library of Congress Catalog Number: 99-90677
ISBN: 0-9673058-0-2

CONTENTS

Acknowledgments

Special thanks to all the women in the first Surrendered Circle, especially Lynnae Bennett and Christine Gordon, who have graciously let me include their work in this book, and who were the first ones brave enough to take this plunge. Without them, I could not have written this book. I'm also grateful to my sisters Hannah and Katie, who let me draft them into surrendering and provided thoughtful insights. Most of all, I'm grateful to my brilliant husband, John Doyle, who made this book possible in every sense of the word.

Introduction

I started practicing the principles of a surrendered wife almost by accident. After years of trying to get my husband to be the way I thought he should be, I had to admit that what I was doing was not making me happy. I read books, went to therapy, talked to other women, and took baby steps towards doing it differently. I was willing to try almost anything because I was lonely in my marriage, and I was exhausted from trying to do everything myself.

As I learned to relinquish control, practiced receiving graciously, and stopped criticizing my husband, something magical happened. The union I had always dreamed of appeared. The man who had wooed me was back.

For our ninth wedding anniversary, I changed my last name to match my husband's. "Now that I know him a little better, I figure I'll give it a shot," I joked to my friends. What I really meant was that I wanted to be intimate with him in a way that I never was before. I wanted to do something that symbolized my tremendous respect for him and to outwardly acknowledge an inward shift. This was the natural development of a path I had started some time ago without realizing it.

The basic principles of a surrendered wife are that she respects her husband's thinking, receives his gifts graciously, tells him what she wants without trying to control him, and relies on her husband to handle household finances. A surrendered wife is vulnerable where she used to be a nag, trusting where she used to be controlling, grateful

"No trumpets sound when

the important decisions of

our life are made. Destiny

is made known silently."

— *Agnes De Mille*

where she used to be dissatisfied, and has faith where she once had doubt. She is abundant where she used to feel impoverished and typically has more disposable income than she did before she surrendered.

Shortly after I started practicing it myself, I had the opportunity to share the philosophy of the surrendered wife with some friends who brought the principles to their marriages. Adding further wonder to the process, these women experienced inspiring transformations. Soon a group of five of us—a Surrendered Circle—was meeting in my living room once a month. The circle grew quickly as women I had never met began calling me to learn more about becoming a surrendered wife. When our size threatened to exceed the capacity of my living room, I closed the meetings to newcomers and started Surrendered Wife workshops. Ever more women came forward wanting to know how to surrender to their husbands.

In the pages of this book, you will see glimpses of stories from the women I know and have met through this process. All the anecdotes are true. Each one is a personal story from a woman who has shared a piece of her journey with me although the names and some other details have been changed to protect privacy.

I wrote this book for women because the responsibility of making the relationship transformation described in this book lies squarely on their shoulders. For best results, *do not discuss what you learn from this book with your husband.* While I do encourage you to discuss *The Surrendered Wife* with other women, talking about it with your mate is counter-productive. I'll explain why later on in the book. For now, just keep in mind that becoming a surrendered wife is much more effective than talking about it.

Surrendering to your husband is not about returning to the fifties or rebelling against feminism. This isn't about women dumbing down or being rigid. It's about being intimate with your husband in a way that's both gratifying and terrifying. It's about having a relationship that brings out the best in both of you and growing together as spiritual beings. It's a proven principle that brings peace, joy, and prosperity for women who employ it.

My sister, Hannah Childs, relates the philosophy of the surrendered wife to her experience as a ballroom dance teacher. In marriage, as with ballroom dancing, she writes that "One must lead and the other must follow. This is not to say that both roles are not equally important. As the famous quote goes, Ginger did everything Fred did and did it backwards and in high heels. In a competition, both people are judged equally, but if they both tried to lead (or follow) it would be a disaster. Instead of working together as a team, they would be pulling each other in opposite directions and would not look graceful or in sync together. In my experience as a teacher, it is rare that I find a woman who doesn't want to 'backlead.' This is such a common occurrence that if you go anywhere to any studio and say the word backlead, they know just what you are talking about."

Whether you have been married for many years or are just starting to date, the philosophy of the surrendered wife will help you find true partnership, incredible romance, passion, and peace. If you are ready to experience a transcending love relationship, read on.

"Love is magical, and it can last, if we remember our differences."

— John Gray

A Surrendered Fairy Tale

Once upon a time there was a small kingdom that was ruled by a wise and generous king. Everyone in the kingdom was prospering and happy and especially grateful for this good king. When the king made a decree, the villagers respected it because they knew the king was acting in their best interests.

One day, the king fell in love with a beautiful, vivacious princess from a neighboring kingdom. The princess was very clever, and she was quite impressed with how well the king ruled his kingdom. She especially loved his wisdom and generosity. The king asked the princess to marry him, and she gladly accepted. Soon she moved into the castle and became the queen. The king was very happy, and he treasured his smart, pretty wife. The queen admired her husband and especially loved to warm-up her cold feet by rubbing them against his perpetually warm feet.

After a while, when the queen had settled in, she noticed that there were just a few things the king could be doing more efficiently. For one thing, she thought he should keep the royal gold in a safer place. Also, she noticed that some of the villagers didn't work as hard as they could, and she was not truly satisfied with the cleanliness of the castle. She went about telling the king how he could improve these things. Anxious to please his queen, the king did his best to correct these situations. At first, the queen seemed satisfied, but, as time went on, she found even more things that she believed he could improve. The king continued to try to make her happy.

About this time, something went awry. The townspeople were not as content and prosperous as they had once been. In fact, they seemed to spend a lot of time fighting amongst themselves. Dismayed with the king's lack of power over his own kingdom, the queen criticized him harshly and came up with even bigger, better plans for how to run the kingdom.

The king began to question his own ability to rule the kingdom at all, and the queen was convinced that he would never be able to keep the castle up to her standards, so she had a second castle built and moved into it. Soon, some villagers were saying the queen knew best how to run the kingdom and that the king should just step down as he couldn't even empty the garbage when it was full. Meanwhile, the king was in a kind of fog, wandering the castle grounds wishing that television would be invented so that he could watch it. Finally, a full-fledged war broke out between the villagers who supported the king and the villagers who thought the queen knew better.

The queen sent out a few royal decrees, but the villagers were still bickering all the time and hardly ever got anything done. As a result of all the non-productivity, the marketplace started to look pretty barren. Things were not going well.

The queen grew tired of all the responsibility and headaches. Everything was one problem after another, and no one seemed the least bit appreciative of what she was doing. The king didn't seem grateful at all! In fact, he seemed rather hostile about the whole thing. Besides, the queen was lonely living in her castle. Most of all, she couldn't seem to get her feet warm! She longed for the days when she and the king would ride a carriage through the kingdom, wave to all the happy peasants, and picnic at the edge of the enchanted forest.

Fortunately, the queen really was a very clever queen, so she came up with a plan. She went to see the king that day to tell him that she wanted to come back to live in his castle. The king welcomed her back, and she set about giving the castle a more feminine touch.

The next day, some of the lords asked her what she intended to do about all the fighting, and she told them the king was handling that now. Understandably, the king was still a bit shell-shocked and wasn't sure what to do. The queen reminded him of what a wonderful job he had been doing running his kingdom before they met and told him she trusted him.

The very next morning, the king thought of a clever plan that would stabilize the economy, reduce inflation, and restore confidence in the marketplace. By the next week, all the financial indicators were positive again.

The queen was very relieved that she didn't have to do everything around the kingdom by herself anymore. She made a public appearance to tell the villagers what great things the king had accomplished. She reminded them of what a wise, generous king he had been. She praised his leadership and said that, as for her, she planned to surrender to the king and do whatever he thought was best. After her rousing speech, everyone had renewed respect for the king and was anxious to hear what he had to say.

From that day onward, the queen made a habit of telling the king her desires like how she wanted to protect the enchanted forest from lumber companies and to keep children from bringing swords to school. Each time, the king would come up with an idea for how to do the things she had spoken about. Sometimes the queen thought the idea was terrific, and sometimes she thought the king's ideas were kind of goofy. Still, she agreed to follow them, knowing that the king had plenty of experience in running a fine kingdom.

The king regained his confidence as a leader; the whole kingdom was more prosperous and peaceful than ever. The villagers were the happiest they had ever been.

Still, there was one small problem in the castle, so the queen told the king that she wanted help getting her feet warm. The king said he would help, and so he did, and they all lived very happily ever after.

What Your Husband Won't Tell You

R-E-S-P-E-C-T

Karen's husband ran a large corporation and earned a six-figure income. A few days before his birthday, he put a note on the counter with the one thing he most wanted his wife to give him: Respect. The same conversation takes place in a variety of forms in households the world over. For many wives, respect is also the hardest thing to give.

Although we don't always say so, many of us think we really know better than our husbands do. From this platform, we can safely criticize everything from their parenting skills to their driving habits. No matter how successful they are, we still believe that they would be better off doing things our way.

In marriage, however, as in nature, water seeks its own level. We marry men who match us, and therefore deserve our respect. Respecting your husband means refraining from comment no matter how much you disapprove of the way he loads the dishwasher. Respect means that when he takes the wrong freeway exit you don't correct him by telling him where to turn. It means that if he keeps going in the wrong direction you will go past the state line and still not correct what he's doing (unless it hurts you physically or spiritually). In fact, no matter what your husband does, you will not try to teach, improve, or correct him. That is the essence of a surrendered wife.

Each time you complain about your husband's dishwashing, driving, or parenting skills, he retracts a little more. He makes a mental note to give up, to some degree, because he can never meet your standards. He may even agree with you subconsciously and retreat from the activity entirely because he thinks you don't want his help or because he fears criticism.

"Wisdom is divided into two parts: (a) having a great deal to say, and (b) not saying it."

— Anonymous

Your husband won't tell you he feels emasculated when you correct his behavior. He won't mention that he feels more like a little boy with his mother than a man with his wife. Naturally, he won't mention how sexually unappealing you are when you act like his mother.

Although he doesn't tell you, on some level you probably know it already. If you're like me, you've often wished you could be more respectful, more trusting of your husband— if only he seemed up to the responsibility. The problem is you'll never know if he really is worthy of your respect until you trust him. That means you'll never experience the joy and relief of being completely vulnerable and relying on him, and he'll never feel the exhilaration and power of knowing you trust him to take care of you–unless you're willing to take this difficult journey.

RECEIVING GRACIOUSLY

I believe in offering women as many choices as possible: education, a satisfying career, full-time motherhood, marriage or any combination of these that fits for her. That's what I think of as feminism—giving more women more choices. I chose to go to college and have a career. I felt so strongly about my identity as a feminist that when I married in my early twenties, I chose not to take my husband's name. Thanks to liberation, I knew my opinion counted, and that I was smart. Unfortunately, I hadn't learned much about the fine art of receiving.

Receiving sounds deceptively easy. It means being open to graciously accepting gifts, however large or small. It means that when your husband offers to put the baby to bed, take you to a show, or get you a chair at the party, you smile sweetly and say thank you. Sounds simple enough, right? In my experience, many women have an agenda that keeps them from being able to accept the things their husbands want to give them. The agendas go something like this:

"Some people find fault as if it were buried treasure."

— *Francis O'Walsh*

"If he puts the baby to bed, he will put the pajamas on backwards again."

"He needs to relax after a long day at work, so I'll put the baby to bed."

"We can't afford to go to a show."

"If he picks the movie, I probably won't like it."

"It would be rude to take the only chair, so I'll stand too."

"I don't want to sit next to that awful woman from the PTA, so I won't take the chair he's offering."

Your opinion does count, and you have every right to express it, but when your husband offers you something, it's in your best interest to accept it graciously and without critical comment. Women are designed to receive both spiritually and sexually. Acknowledging this will not undo what women have gained politically and socially through liberation, but practicing it will make your marriage more intimate and fulfilling.

If you are thinking you would be thrilled if your husband offered to do anything for you, chances are you are overlooking his gifts. In my experience, a woman will often dismiss her husband's gifts if they aren't what she has in mind. If you feel that your husband rarely offers anything, I'd encourage you to open your eyes a little wider. You may be surprised to find out that you've been overlooking his

"The art of acceptance is the art of making someone who has just done you a small favor wish that he might have done you a greater one."

— *Russell Lynes*

offers and therefore not receiving them.

Roxanne and Rich are one example of this. When I first encouraged Roxanne to concentrate on receiving from her husband, she scoffed, complaining that he never lifted a finger to do anything for her. She told me it was an ongoing struggle to get him to bathe the kids at night or hand her a diaper. Even the smallest request was met with groans and unwillingness. During the course of our conversation, however, she mentioned the two bathing suits Rich had gotten her for Mother's Day. Later, she told me he had also offered to put her up at a hotel for the weekend so she could catch up on her sleep. By the time she started complaining about how he had left some spots on the windows when he washed her car, I was on to her. She was completely overlooking her husband's gifts because they weren't the gifts she thought he should be giving her!

Roxanne is a very bright and enlightened woman, and she is certainly not alone in her myopia about her own husband. I've met many other wives who have the same distorted view of their mates. Until someone else pointed out their husband's generosity, they just couldn't see it themselves.

When we don't receive our husband's gifts, we feel deprived because we think he never does anything for us. We want him to give us things, so we go about trying to get him to offer us the things we think he should be giving us. We write notes, set boundaries, or say how we feel to get him to change. Usually, he responds poorly, dragging his feet and making it clear he considers the task a big chore. By this time, we are convinced that he is inconsiderate and lazy. Even if he does what we want, we are still unhappy because we don't just want him to give us gifts; we want him to *want* to give us gifts.

To better understand this idea, imagine yourself preparing a gift for a close friend. You've thought long and worked hard to make sure this gift is just what your friend will like. You lovingly wrap the gift and with great anticipation, you present it to your friend. But instead of smiling happily and thanking you, your friend rolls her eyes and refuses the gift. When you ask her why she won't accept the gift, she says she just doesn't want it or that you didn't offer it the right way. Naturally, you would be very disappointed. You would certainly think twice before getting a present for this friend again, and you might stop giving her things altogether.

If you recognize yourself in this situation, don't worry—all is not lost. As long as you are still married, there is an easy cure for this problem. Most husbands continue to offer their wives small gifts even after years of being rebuffed. Start receiving graciously and the gifts will multiply and come with greater enthusiasm almost immediately.

Receiving graciously means that even if the gift is not exactly what you want, you smile and say thank you. For instance, if you want a new car, and your husband gets you one that's better than your current car but not as good as the Mercedes you had your eye on, accept it graciously. Even when what you're receiving is not as much as you want, be grateful for what you have.

In a situation where the husband is truly withholding from his wife, there is a very real possibility that he's reacting to repeated rejection and ongoing emasculation. The cure for this is also quite simple and works quickly. This will be discussed in another chapter. In the meantime, practice receiving your husband's gifts the way your mother taught you to accept a compliment: smile sweetly and say, "thank you."

CONTROLLING WIVES AND HOW WE GOT THIS WAY

Before she fell in love and got married, every controlling wife had parents who let her down in some respect.

Prescription to alleviate feelings of lack

Make a point of graciously receiving everything your husband offers you, no matter how large or small. Even if you're not sure you want the gift or think he can't afford it. Be on the lookout for gifts you might not have noticed before.

"Treat people as if they were what they ought to be, and you help them to become what they are capable of being."

— Goethe

It may have been in little ways like not buying her the tennis shoes she needed to fit in at school. It may have also been in big ways like an ongoing addiction to alcohol that made her parent altogether unavailable. At a young age, some of our most basic needs went unmet. We then made an erroneous conclusion: The more we could control, the better. We decided that no one would ever really take care of us the way we wanted them to. We even embraced a childish belief that if we were always in charge, things were more likely to go our way. Some of us were so used to living in fear about not getting what we needed; we never even noticed our quicker pulse and shallow breathing. We normalized this level of terror and our accompanying autoresponse: control.

When Amy talked about her husband, she explained to me that there is always a reason she needs to control his actions. The reason he should eat less red meat is because it's better for his health. The reason he should take one route to the city and not the other is because it would save time and hassle. The reason he should install the curtains her way is because it's more efficient. The real "reason" Amy can't stop controlling her husband is because she's terrified that if she lets go of the steering wheel for a minute, her needs will go unmet. Telling her husband how to do things provides her with the illusion of safety, but the reality is lonely.

My own terror was so strong that I had great difficulty going with my husband on what we called the "no-control date." My therapist encouraged me to experiment with the concept of trusting my husband by agreeing to go out with him on a date where he made all the decisions. On this particular date, he was to tell me how to dress and what time to be ready. He would also drive, pick a restaurant, order for me, pick up the check and plan any other activities for the evening.

I did so poorly with this experiment that by the time we were on the road, I had already figured out where he was taking me and I was giving him instructions on where to turn. At the restaurant, I told him where to park and squirmed anxiously in my chair as he ordered the dinner I had strategically mentioned appealed to me.

The service that night was abominable. The food took much longer than it should have, and the waitress ignored us completely. I told my husband I would ask to speak to the manager and get him to give us our dinners for free because of the extraordinary wait. He assured me we were in no hurry and that he was happy to pay for the dinner. He even poured gasoline on the fire by saying he was just enjoying the opportunity to sit and talk with me! I was beside myself with fear and discomfort. When we finally left the restaurant, I begged him to please take me home instead of to the movies—all because I was so terrified.

"Some women work so hard to make good husbands that they never manage to make good wives."

— Anonymous

At no point during the evening was I in any danger of being hurt, embarrassed, bored, deprived, or even having to eat something I didn't like. But to see how I acted, you might have thought I was going before a firing squad. That's how big my fear was.

In reality, I was with a man who knows me well and wants me to be happy. My terror had nothing to do with him. In fact, I was terrified of being out of control long before I met him. I was so accustomed to control that I often did it without even realizing I was doing it. Finally, I learned to dig a little deeper when my urge to control came up and simply say that I was afraid. Unfortunately, this was only a little better in terms of healing my relationship and restoring intimacy.

TERRIFIED IS AN UNDERSTATEMENT

To respect your husband, first acknowledge that your terror is not about him. With this in mind, I suggest

Prescription for alleviating overwhelm

Go out with your husband on a date where he makes all the decisions without consulting you. If you find yourself trying to control his actions, ask yourself what it is you are afraid will happen.

that you stop controlling him or telling him about how much the things he does or says scare you. As much as you think it's his behavior that you're scared about, it most likely is not. I'm not suggesting that you just ignore your feelings. Your fear is real, and you need to be able to express it. Instead of telling your husband about your fears related to him, call a girlfriend and complain all you want about how nervous you get when he follows the car in front of him too closely. Feel free to tell your mother that you're afraid he's not going to pay the bills on time. Let loose with your sister about how concerned you are that he's not following the doctor's orders. Just don't express your fears *about* him *to* him, and make sure your confidante is also sworn to secrecy. This information must never get back to him.

The reasoning for this is simple: People tend to live up to our expectations for them. If you make it clear to your husband that you expect him to screw up at work, wreck the car, or neglect his health, you are setting a negative expectation. Just as you would not tell your children that you're afraid they'll do poorly in school, don't tell your husband about your negative expectations.

Here are the kinds of things wives frequently say to their husbands that set up negative expectations:

"Don't you think we should slow down a little?"

"This is not where you're supposed to turn."

"You have to rinse the dishes before you put them in the dishwasher."

"We're not going to have enough money to pay the bills this month."

"Why don't you just call a plumber?"

At best, what most husbands would hear in these examples is, "I know better than you do how to handle this situation." Even worse, they might hear, "You're not smart enough to figure this out for yourself."

Besides the potential damage of having a negative expectation, you are also wasting your breath. If you take an honest look at your relationship, you will realize that you have never really accomplished anything positive through control. Chances are he doesn't spend any more time with the kids, drive any slower, or eat any better than he did before you started telling him what to do and how to do it.

WHEN TO STOP SURRENDERING AND GET OUT

Your husband does things that get on your very last nerve. I know this because I have a husband myself, and, like yours, he is a mere mortal man with numerous imperfections. At times I found his shortcomings so big they seemed unlivable. I don't feel this way now, but in retrospect, it didn't take much for me to feel that way before. As it turns out, my husband is one of the good guys. But how do you know if your husband is a good guy? What if he really isn't right for you?

There are some circumstances where I would suggest separation or divorce as opposed to surrendering. If your husband is physically abusive or has an active addiction, he can't be trusted. You are the only one who can make these judgment calls, so here are some guidelines that will help you decide whether or not your husband is worth respecting.

1. Do not surrender to a man who is physically abusive to you. This does not mean a man who seems like he might *become* physically abusive, or one who hits tables or walls. I also would discount incidents where you were physically abusive to *him* and he reacted in defense. However, if your husband has hit, kicked or punched you in anger, I urge you to leave that relationship as quickly as possible. If he has physically forced you to be sexual against your will, leave at once. When your safety is threatened, there can be no intimacy. Get help from friends, ther-

"If you keep on saying things are going to be bad, you have a good chance of being a prophet."

— Isaac Bashevis Singer

apists or clergy and get out. Start making plans and taking action *today*.

2. Do not surrender to a man who is physically abusive to your children. If your husband is inappropriately violent or sexual with your kids, I urge you to take action to protect them immediately. The sooner you leave this relationship, the better your chances of getting into a relationship with a healthy, loving man who will *protect*, rather than *harm*, you and your children. (Spanking a child as discipline, however controversial or unacceptable to you, does not qualify as physical abuse. Just because the two of you disagree about corporal punishment does not give you justification to leave the relationship.)

3. Do not surrender to a husband who has an active addiction. A man with an addiction to a substance such as alcohol or drugs, or to an activity such as gambling or sex with other women cannot be trusted. I can offer little hope of intimacy in this situation, as he will always serve his addiction before your safety and happiness.

Only you know if your husband falls into one of these categories. If you are uncertain, but suspect that he has an active addiction, find some quiet time and space to contemplate this question. Ask your gut, and listen to the response. Remind yourself that you deserve to be the first priority to your husband, but be careful not to make a case where there isn't one.

For instance, a past extramarital affair does not automatically make your husband a sex addict. It may have been his inappropriate reaction to years of emasculation and criticism from his wife. That doesn't make the affair your fault; it's still his responsibility to keep his vows. Your marriage can heal completely from this type of infidelity once you begin surrendering if your husband is willing to recommit himself to monogamy.

On the other hand, a chronically unfaithful man who

"Confidence is contagious. So is lack *of confidence."*

— *Michael O'Brien*

has promised many times to stop cheating–but doesn't–is not a viable partner in an intimate marriage. I classify this behavior as a sexual addiction, which makes him untrustworthy. Only you know what kind of man your husband is. Trust your gut in making this judgment, and remember that the sooner you reject what is inappropriate for you, the sooner you will be able to form a relationship with someone who will treat you like a princess.

If your husband doesn't fall into one of the categories above, however, then you are married to one of the good guys. Not a perfect husband, but one who is capable of loving you and cherishing you. Really.

EVEN GOOD GUYS FORGET TO PUT THEIR SOCKS IN THE HAMPER

In my experience, women who fear intimacy tend to have a hair-trigger response to events in their marriage. One woman described herself as having her bags packed and her running shoes on at all times so she could leave at the slightest provocation. My therapist reminded me that when I first started coming to see her, I had the same mindset. I started out by letting her know that I was ready to hear the truth and that if I had married the wrong man and needed to get a divorce, I would do that. Today my friends laugh at me when I tell them this. What was I thinking?

I was terrified that I would never get what I wanted in a relationship, which was to be treasured, pampered, supported, protected, and loved. Of course I wasn't getting what I wanted at that time because I had adopted such a defensive posture. Perhaps you have done the same thing.

As an analogy, imagine that at the end of a date that instead of standing there ready to receive a kiss, you stood with your arms crossed and glared at your date. It would take a pretty brave or very inconsiderate man to kiss you under those circumstances. If you've ever uttered the words, "Never mind! I'll do it myself!" or even worse,

"Try to want what you have, instead of spending your strength trying to get what you want."

— Abraham L. Feinberg

taken action that screamed out that sentiment, you have metaphorically stood there with your fists up when it was time for the goodnight kiss.

In other words, just because your husband throws his dirty socks on the floor instead of in the hamper does not mean that you need to divorce him. Even if you think he's verbally abusive. Even if he is grouchy and hurts your feelings all the time. Even if he ignores the kids and does nothing but watch television or work all the time.

Even if you think he's not meeting any of your needs, and that you'd be better off alone, I urge you to stay and work on this relationship. Remember the sanctity of your vows. The part you contribute to a failed marriage will follow you into every future relationship until you get some healing. Resolve to stop the cycle here, and take the action necessary to have a healthy relationship with the man you're with. Other women who have come before you managed to do it even though they thought it was impossible. As long as your husband does not fall into one of the three categories above, you too can have a healthy, fulfilling relationship.

If you are like most women, you are already thinking of reasons that it isn't possible for you to stop controlling your husband. Perhaps you feel you cannot refrain from teaching or correcting your husband because of the children, or because of the finances, or because he is such a loser. If you are thinking there is some reason you can't follow this suggestion, you are not alone. That's what we all think.

The truth is, it is possible for you to respect your husband. I know what I'm suggesting is difficult. I assure you that the incredible intimacy and relief you will feel as a result are well worth it. Through this narrow doorway, you will find the kind of relationship you've always dreamed was possible.

"Rare is the person who can weigh the faults of others without his thumb on the scale."

— *Byron Langfeld*

CHAPTER

2

He Doesn't Have to Change, But You Do

Many wives believe that their husband is just not capable in some vital regard such as parenting, managing finances, or self-care. This belief comes from our own fear: a fear that was probably fully developed before we even met our husbands. As a result, there are lots of women running around with wonderful husbands that they don't appreciate or even really see. If you are such a woman, you are certainly not alone.

I had a conversation with a woman who was complaining that she had to pay the bills at her house even though she hated the task. When I suggested that she relinquish the responsibility to her husband, she explained that although he was very successful in his business, her husband somehow was not up to the task of putting checks in the proper envelopes and mailing them once a month. As ridiculous as this sounds, I have spoken to many women who have similar illogical beliefs about their husbands. Some women say they are afraid to leave the children with their own father while they go out. Still others doubt their husband's ability to plan an enjoyable evening out or negotiate a good deal on a car.

We have good reasons to cling to our absurd fallacies. One advantage of concentrating on your husband's

"Each of us has his own little private conviction of rightness and almost by definition, the Utopian condition of which we all dream is that in which all people finally see the error of their ways and agree with us."

— *S.I. Hayakawa*

faults is that you never really have to do the scariest thing of all: trust him completely. If you tell yourself that your husband is incapable, you don't have to give up control. By focusing your energy on his problems, you can ignore your own shortcomings. This is why so many of us have convinced ourselves that *he* is the one who has all the bad habits. We reason that *he* is the unpleasant or incompetent one in the family.

The truth is, your husband may be unpleasant or incompetent, but until you give him your complete trust over a sustained period of time, you can't be sure. He may be a great guy who spends most of his time defending himself against your criticism. Until you stop emasculating him, you'll never know what it's like to be truly *married* to your husband.

I am *not* saying that you are responsible for his actions. Your husband is always completely responsible for his own actions. If he is a poor father or neglects his family, that is *not* his wife's fault. At the same time, if you are nagging, undermining, criticizing or disrespecting him, you are making his job more difficult. You're not responsible for what he does, but you certainly influence him.

You might argue that he influences you too. You could say, as I have before, that if he would stop being so obnoxious or stupid, you would act differently. Perhaps you think someone should write a book for men explaining how they can be more responsible husbands. Perhaps someone should. Of course, you couldn't make your husband read it, or do what it says, so you're only chance of improving your marriage is to change your behavior. I'm reminded of the Serenity Prayer:

God, grant me the serenity to accept the things I cannot change [like my husband]
The courage to change the things I can [like myself]
And the wisdom to know the difference [between

him and me].

I know it doesn't seem fair. It didn't seem fair to me that I had to work so hard to change while my husband continued to sit around watching television. If it's any comfort, I can tell you that your husband will have to make big changes too. In fact, he will have to transform in order to stay in step with you as you take the spiritual journey of trusting him. He will have to rise to new levels to meet this remarkable occasion, particularly if you have never fully trusted him before. He will have to listen to his own inner voice of conviction instead of relying on yours to tell him when he's not doing something right. He will need to use his own mind to figure out what's best for his family as opposed to carrying out your subtle or not-so-subtle orders. He will be taking on far more responsibility than he ever has before. He will make all those changes as soon as you begin practicing the principles of the surrendered wife.

"There's always room for improvement, you know-- it's the biggest room in the house."

— Louise Heath Leber

TURN DOWN YOUR VOLUME TO LISTEN

My husband once told me about a couple he saw while he was waiting his turn for a haircut. While the barber was trying his best to cut the man's hair, his wife was standing by giving the barber very explicit instructions. "Not too short in the back," she told him, "and make sure it doesn't stick out on the top!"

Several other men were waiting for haircuts as well, and when the barber finished and the couple left, everyone sighed with relief. My husband got in the chair next and told the barber, "My wife couldn't come today, so you're on your own."

Even though I recognized myself in this story, I was not able to change my behavior. I couldn't seem to keep from talking on my husband's behalf or making decisions for him. I told myself that it was a good thing I did, or he would never do anything. It seemed like he just waited for me to decide what we should do, and sort of dragged his feet once I did.

As you can imagine, what I was doing was talking all the time so that my husband couldn't get a word in edgewise. I had lots of opinions, and I knew what should be done and how it should be done, just like the wife at the barbershop.

There are many different ways to be controlling, and I've probably tried them all. Sometimes I would change from one method that I *knew* was disrespectful to something that seemed subtler. For instance, instead of saying something downright critical, I would give my husband a disapproving look. This seemed less offensive to me, but not to him. When I tried to stop giving him 'the look,' I started asking questions that seemed innocent enough but clearly conveyed my disapproval. (i.e., You're going to wear *that*?) I would try to explain to my husband what *I* would do if I were in his situation, hoping that he would do what I thought he should. I've made countless unsolicited suggestions, gasped in the car while he was driving, and frowned at the lettuce he bought, all in the desperate, futile attempt to control his actions.

When I was doing this, I was like a loud speaker with the volume set to "10." My husband's volume was never louder than mine, so I could rarely hear him. It wasn't until I turned down the volume on my speaker substantially that I started to notice he was making any sounds at all.

In that regard, it was up to me to change first. For so long, I thought that he needed to take more initiative, not let people walk all over him, to SPEAK UP. Ironically, as soon as I was willing to turn my speaker down, he seemed to change immediately. Imagine my surprise when, after all those years of begging and manipulating and cajoling him to speak up, I discovered the problem had actually been that I couldn't hear him over my own noise.

Prescription for wives of husbands who never want to talk

Spend the evening listening to your husband. Even if neither of you talks much, make a point of really hearing everything he says. Smile and invite him to say more by tilting your head and saying, "Really?" or "Oh?", then LISTEN.

So how do you turn down the volume? I joke about needing a lot of duct tape around my house so I can roll it around and around my mouth. Otherwise, it's not easy keeping things from coming out of it that I'll later wish I hadn't said. In other words, be quiet. At least a few times a day, hold your tongue when you would normally speak. Listen for what comes out of your husband when you are silent.

ASK FOR WHAT YOU WANT

Imagine you go to a restaurant and look at a menu. The waitress wants to take your order, but instead of asking her to bring you a certain dish on the menu, you begin telling her how to prepare chicken. You start by telling her how to clean the chicken properly, then how to season it, and how much of each ingredient to use. You tell her how to cook it, and for how long, and how to garnish it so it will be appetizing. Naturally, the restaurant staff would probably find you pretty irritating. Even if they did follow your instructions, they'd probably also spit in the food before they brought it to your table because nobody wants to be told how to do his job.

Imagine another scenario: You go into a restaurant, and when the waitress asks to take your order, you say, "I think you know," or "Can't you see I'm hungry?" At best, the waitress could suggest that you order the special, or she could choose something off the menu at random and bring it to you. Chances are slim that your dinner would be what you prefer.

Fortunately, most of us go into a restaurant and tell the waitress what we want without telling her how to do it. This works beautifully. The waitress brings the order to the cook who prepares the dish to our liking, and she brings it to us. Everybody is happy.

I have discovered that this same system works very

"The only thing worse than a husband who never notices what you cook or what you wear, is a husband who always notices what you cook and what you wear."

— Sandra Litoff

"If we lose affection and

kindness from our life,

we've lost all that gives it

charm."

— *Cicero*

well in my marriage. If I tell my husband I want something, he works to get it for me as best he can. If I tell him how I want him to do it, he generally doesn't do it at all. And if I don't tell him, he has no idea what I want and so generally doesn't give it to me.

Just as you don't need to explain to the waitress why you want a certain dish, you don't have to explain to your husband why you want what you want. It is not necessary to say, "I want the apricot chicken because chicken is not as fatty as beef, and I like chicken with a sweet sauce on it, plus I like the vegetables that come with it, and I've had the chicken here before and it's not too dry." The waitress might listen politely, but she would probably just wish you would stop talking so she can get on with her job. By the same token, you don't need to say, "I want to get a new dress because all of my old ones are worn out, and it's been three years since I bought anything new for myself, and I saved $40 on groceries with coupons last month." You can just say, "I want a new dress."

A surrendered wife never hesitates to tell her husband what she wants. When you say to your husband, "I want a new dress," or "I want another baby," or "I want a bigger house," you are giving him a new opportunity to feel accomplished and proud about how happy he makes you.

Notice, however, that these examples are all end-results. Expressing the desire for a new dress is very different from telling him to go to the department store and buy you a blue dress for your birthday. Asking for another baby is far different from telling him he needs to wear looser underwear to keep his sperm count up. Asking for a bigger house is a lot different than telling him to ask for a raise so the two of you can afford one. Do you see the difference? I'm suggesting that you tell him the end result, but not specify how it happens, just as you would tell the waitress what you want without telling her how to make it.

Before you tell him what it is you want, think about it carefully and make sure you are asking for an end-result, not what you think he should do to achieve it. For instance, if you want to own a home you would say, "I want to buy a house." You would not say, "I want you to put in some overtime so we can save up a down-payment." You should also try to avoid giving a lengthy explanation, like "I want a new house because this one is so small it is absolutely driving me nuts! I'm sick of having to live in such cramped quarters. Plus, I think the neighborhood is going down hill..."

"Eating words has never given me indigestion."

— Winston Churchill

Remember that as with anything in life, you can't always get what you want. Sometimes your husband will say no, or not now. Sometimes he'll give you what you say you want, but it won't be quite what you had in mind. Regardless of how far short of your expectations his offering is, your job is to receive it graciously. Graciousness means never mentioning that the gift is not quite 'good enough.'

IN AN EMERGENCY, BREAK DOWN AND APOLOGIZE

Fortunately for me and other women I know, you don't have to surrender perfectly to enjoy some of the marvelous effects on your marriage. It is important, however, to apologize when you realize you haven't been so perfect. A critical aspect of surrendering is catching yourself as soon as you can and letting him know that you realize you were disrespectful and that you're sorry.

In the beginning, you will probably find yourself having to apologize a lot: every time you roll your eyes at his idea, make an unsolicited suggestion about what he's wearing, or tell him what to say on the phone. This may be frustrating, but it is necessary. Even if you don't feel sorry, do your best to apologize when you are critical, bossy, nagging, dismissing, or contradictory. This will feel odd and, perhaps, even dishonest. Still, I suggest that you take this leap and act as if you do respect your husband. The more you act like a respectful wife, the more likely you are to see the things about your husband that are worth respecting.

When you apologize, be sure to reference the specific situation. For instance, you might say, "I apologize for being disrespectful when I criticized the way you were helping Taylor with her homework." Next, allow him to respond and do your best not to say anything further about the original point of contention. In some cases, this may require putting large quantities of duct tape around your mouth. Do whatever it takes.

The temptation to comment on the original situation will be enormous. From your point of view, the comment may seem perfectly innocent. For instance, you might be tempted to follow up the apology by saying, "It's just that you need to be a little more patient with 6-year-olds." If you say that, guess what? You were just disrespectful again. Now you owe him ANOTHER apology, so you're no better off than when you first started the conversation.

Still, it's important that you listen to his response after you apologize and acknowledge that you heard him by saying, "uh-huh," or "okay." You might even repeat yourself by saying, "Yeah, I'm really sorry about that." To the best of your ability, don't offer anything more about this topic.

When I first suggested that she apologize for being disrespectful to her husband, Emily balked. She asked, "Do I have to use the word disrespectful?" I encouraged her to try it just this once. According to Emily, she mumbled the dreaded word when she delivered her line, but it didn't matter. Her husband had a tender smile for her when he said, "I love seeing this side of you."

THE HIGH COST OF DOING IT ALL

Most controlling wives are used to doing everything

> **Prescription for improving marital tranquillity**
>
> **Think of something you said or did recently that was disrespectful to your husband and apologize for that specific incident. Listen and acknowledge his response without further comment.**

by themselves and think their husbands are too lazy and in-considerate to help them. As a result of the pressure of try-ing to do it all, they frequently feel tired and stressed. They then try to get their husbands to help by screaming "Help out once in a while!" The husband jumps up to do some-thing with the primary motivation of avoiding further abuse. With this source of motivation, he is not likely to do anymore than the absolute minimum requirement. The wife is dissatisfied with his efforts and tells herself it's easier to just do it herself. She feels more alone than ever, and the husband is reminded that the woman who knows him best in the world finds him entirely inadequate. He returns to his distant, protective semi-coma, and both are worse off for the exchange.

  If this is a familiar scenario, practice saying these words: I can't. A surrendered wife is quick to admit when she can't do something and ask for help. This is entirely different from barking orders. For example:

> Controlling: *Why don't you carry our toddler into the house?*
> Surrendered: *I can't carry him. I need help.*

> Controlling: *You try paying the bills around here. It's not easy!*
> Surrendered: *Paying the bills is making me nuts. I can't do it anymore.*

> Controlling: *You better get on the phone and get a plumber down here.*
> Surrendered: *There's something wrong with the plumbing, and I don't know what to do. What do you think?*

You could argue that you CAN handle these situa-

"To put the world right in order, we must first put the nation in order; to put the nation in order, we must first put the family in order; to put the family in order, we must first cultivate our personal life; we must first set our hearts right."

— Confucius

"When a man does not feel

loved just the way he is, he

will either consciously or

unconsciously repeat the

behavior that is not being

accepted. He feels an inner

compulsion to repeat the

behavior until he feels

loved and accepted."

— John Gray

tions and you DO know what to do. Before you say that, consider the cost. If you've been doing everything yourself for a while, you're probably feeling angry, lonely, and tired. So you CAN do everything if you're willing to be frazzled and edgy all the time. You may even be experiencing headaches, frequent illness, back problems, or other physical symptoms as a result of the overload.

If you want to be intimate with your husband and have more free-time and relaxation, you really CAN'T do it all. From this moment forward, pay special attention to anything that makes you cranky and start admitting that you just can't do it. Maybe you never could. Sadly, you've probably been doing things for years that have cost you too much.

If going around saying you can't do things sounds like a nutty suggestion to you, you are certainly not alone. The typical controlling wife is used to bucking up, persevering, and toughing it out no matter what the cost. She doesn't appear to *need* help. She is certainly not used to risking rejection by *asking* for help or being vulnerable. She is none too keen on revealing her weakness. However, when she does take this tack, her husband sees an opportunity to be the hero, to carry his delicate wife over the proverbial mud puddle, and win her enduring adoration and gratitude. This is a far cry from the motivation he'll feel about doing something to get you off of his back.

You may wonder if this approach will actually work with your husband. Remember that he is probably no exception. As an example, consider the results of a gag from an episode of Candid Camera.

The set-up was a woman who was walking around with one shoe off and limping badly, barely able to walk. She approached some unsuspecting men and asked them to help her get where she was going. One of the men she approached--a stranger--actually picked her up and carried her to her destination. The Candid Camera crew tried it again with another man, and again the man picked her up and carried her. They tried this plan about 15 times, and each time a different man carried the woman to her destination. These men were every size, age, shape, and race, and all of them had the same response to a damsel in distress.

Is your husband really so different than the men captured by the Candid Camera? You will never know until you show your weakness and risk rejection by admitting your limitations and asking for help.

DON'T CROWD THE SETTER

I love to play volleyball, and when I play, I love to be the setter. The setter is the player who receives the ball from a passer and puts it up high enough for the hitter to pound it over the net. As a general rule, the setter always gets the second ball unless she calls for help. This rule keeps people from crashing into each other or letting the ball hit the ground unnecessarily.

Inexperienced players sometimes worry that the setter won't be able to get to the ball in time. They try to "help" by standing under the ball so that they can set it if necessary. This is called crowding the setter. I hate when that happens because when I try to set the ball, I've got someone standing in my way. I might even drop the ball because of the interference. When this happens, the inexperienced player will sometimes turn around and say, "Why didn't you call for help? I could have gotten it!"

Indeed!

If the rookie had stayed out of my way, I would have given her a beautiful set and the satisfaction of pounding it over the net and into the other team. Instead, she was too busy crowding the setter—worrying that I wasn't going to do my job and then blaming me when I couldn't get past her. Did I mention I *hate* when that happens?

"We have been taught to believe that negative equals realistic and positive equals unrealistic."

— Susan Jeffers

"You gain strength,

courage and confidence by

every experience in which

you really stop to look fear

in the face...You must do

the thing you think you

cannot do."

— Eleanor Roosevelt

So what does this long story about volleyball have to do with surrendering to your husband? Just that if you worry that your husband won't do what he's supposed to and stand in his way under the pretense of being ready to help him, you're really making his job much harder. You're also dragging your team down, and you're blaming the wrong person for your troubles. Don't crowd the setter. If your husband is supposed to take care of something, let him take care of it—even if you think he can't do it, or he'll be late, or he'll have to pay extra. If you get in the way and he drops the ball, you'll only have yourself to blame. Quit worrying about him and stay focused on yourself.

Even if you're not saying anything to your husband, you can still crowd him by putting a lot of energy into what he's doing. Checking on the pile of bills to see what he's paid—even when he's not around—is a form of crowding the setter. Worrying that he hasn't called so-and-so, being on alert in case he asks you where to turn, and throwing him a look that says he shouldn't have said something are all examples of crowding the setter.

I know this idea sounds bizarre, but I assure you that your husband can read you like a book. Not surprisingly, he knows what you're thinking even if you don't say it. He is familiar with your expressions and body language, so he can sense when your energy is all over what he's doing. Therefore you need to keep your energy to yourself so he has the space to do his job.

The best way to stay out of trouble in this regard is to practice replacing your current fearful thoughts with a gratitude list. For instance, when you find yourself thinking "His clothes don't match!" replace that thought by listing all the things in your life that you're grateful for. Put your list down on paper whenever possible. If you're somewhere without a pen and paper or time to write, at least go through your gratitudes mentally. Here's how my gratitude list looks.

Today I'm grateful for my:

- Husband
- House
- Health
- Adorable nephew
- Brother and sisters
- Friends
- Car
- Computer
- New hutch
- Clients
- Sushi lunch
- Housecleaner
- Pint of Ben & Jerry's ice cream in freezer
- Cute clothes to wear
- Beautiful bedspread
- Manicure and pedicure
- Flexible schedule

At first, you may have trouble writing a gratitude list. You might go to write down something that you're grateful for but think of something else that you *wish* you had. For instance, you might start to say you're grateful for your car, but then stop to think about how it really needs to be serviced. Instead of finding the negatives in your gratitude list, just stay focused on what it is you're grateful about in your life in this moment. It can be anything--nice weather, your cat, weekends. The point is to remember that just for today, you're absolutely fine. In fact, you're better than fine--you've got lots to be grateful for. Concentrate on that and you'll soon forget about whatever it is you were worrying about for your husband. If you start obsessing about him again when you get done listing everything you can think of, start the gratitude list over and repeat as necessary.

"If a woman can only succeed by emulating men, I think it is a great loss and not a success. The aim is not only for a woman to succeed, but to keep her womanhood and let her womanhood influence society."

— Suzanne Brogger

"Oh, I'm scared all the

time! I just act as if I'm

not."

— Katherine Hepburn

Making a gratitude list helps to combat controlling thoughts by addressing your fears, which are the root of control. If you can remind yourself that you are perfectly okay right this moment, you can begin to relinquish the control. Even better, you can enjoy that very moment you were going to spend worrying about something that's out of your control. Since life is made up of lots of little moments, taking this one step could make your whole life a lot more enjoyable. Not only that, you'll be giving the setter enough space to put the volleyball up in the air so the hitter can slam it over the net. Did I mention I love when that happens?

Why Are We Whispering?

The key to a good marriage is good communication, right? I've heard that over and over again. To me, this meant that I told my husband every feeling and thought that I had, including when I thought he was wrong, when I felt nervous with his driving, and when I didn't approve of his appearance. I was just communicating, and if some communication is good, more communication is better, right? The truth is, there are some things you are better off keeping to yourself.

If you are like me, your first instinct will be to tell your husband everything you've learned about the practices of a surrendered wife or even to hand him the book so he can read it himself. Instead, I urge you to *consider keeping this new information to yourself.* The idea of keeping secrets from your husband may sound counter to the whole concept of being intimate. After all, how can you expect to be truly connected and understand each other if you don't share all your feelings?

The key to feeling connected with another human being has a great deal to do with feeling safe. We feel safe when we know we're not going to be criticized, dismissed, ridiculed, or insulted. So part of being intimate is being very careful never to criticize, dismiss, ridicule, or insult

If you can't say something

nice, don't say anything at

all.

— *Mom*

your husband, right? Yet here are some of the things I've heard bright, thoughtful women say to their husbands when they're newly surrendered:

"I'm really afraid you're not going to do it right, but it says in this book I should let you take over the checkbook."

"I'm supposed to start respecting you more, according to this book."

"This author says I shouldn't give you advice. I don't think that's right, do you?"

"I'm going to start surrendering because I'm sick of doing everything around here!"

"According to this book, I'm supposed to just keep my mouth shut even when you do the dishes wrong."

"From now on, I'm going to appreciate your little gifts."

"I'm going to pretend I respect you and believe in you, even when I don't."

"You have to take over the checkbook now."

Each of these comments is an inherent criticism or subtle attempt to control. Defense, not intimacy, would be a natural reaction, yet this is difficult to see in our own relationships. Perhaps you would not make this mistake, but others who have come before you have certainly struggled with it. For this reason, do not discuss anything about surrendered wives with your husband, at least for now.

I'm making a special plea for your discretion in this matter because I've noticed a common tendency among wives to disregard this suggestion. Some women tell me that they *know* they weren't supposed to tell their husbands about it, but their husband is different, or they themselves are different, or they always share everything with their husband.

Surrendering to your husband is going to change your whole life, and it's going to change his too, but talking about it and doing it are not at all the same thing. Withholding information from your husband may feel dishonest, but it's in your best interest to keep this information to yourself for now.

When Paula first surrendered she was feeling especially uncomfortable with 'keeping secrets' from her husband although she was seeing remarkable changes in her marriage. I suggested that she plan to tell her husband what she was doing, but only after she'd been doing it for at least six months. She agreed, and when six months had past, Paula had transformed. She no longer felt so much judgment towards her husband, and she realized there really wasn't any secret to tell. Her husband knew she had changed and didn't seem the least bit betrayed that she hadn't told him what she was doing sooner. He even knew it had something to do with being a surrendered wife, and which of her friends were involved in surrendering.

You may be tempted to ask your husband how he likes the "new you" or if he's noticed anything different lately. It's human nature to want some positive reinforcement. However, your husband is not the appropriate person to ask for such reinforcement. Although you are doing a lot of hard work, you can't really ask your husband to gush about how you haven't been controlling or rude to him in a while.

Remember that, at a minimum, your husband has every right to expect you to treat him with dignity and respect, even if you weren't doing that before. You wouldn't ask your boss if he's noticed that you've been coming to work every day for the past few months because that's a minimum requirement of most jobs. Likewise, don't ask your husband if he's noticed you're not as controlling and critical. You know you're improving, and you can get feedback and accolades from other women about your progress. Remember that the intimacy and joy in your marriage is the

"The voluntary path to cheerfulness, if our spontaneous cheerfulness be lost, is to sit up cheerfully, and act and speak as if cheerfulness were already there. To feel brave, act as if we were brave, use all our will to that end, and courage will very likely replace fear."

— William James

reward that you're really after.

GET READY TO THANK THE ACADEMY

"Won't my husband know there's something going on?" women often ask me. Of course he will! Most husbands are very aware of their wife's moods and habits. He will notice that something has changed and be pleasantly surprised to find that his wife is treating him respectfully, and seems more appreciative and happier. In general, he will know that you're easier to live with. In turn, he too will probably seem easier to live with; however, he's not likely to come out and ask you what you're up to.

For one thing, while you may feel you're changing dramatically on your end, the changes may not be as noteworthy to him. Habits change incrementally over time, and sometimes a gradual change feels like no change at all until you look back to compare. Since surrendering to your husband is more about the absence of an old behavior, it's likely to take a while before your husband notices. Initially, he may be waiting for the other shoe to drop. Eventually, he will start to trust in your new behavior.

There's another reason your husband probably won't ask you why you're behaving differently. If he's used to waiting to find out what to do from you, and you stop barking orders, he's going to get reacquainted with his own voice. This is the same voice that told him he was attracted to you, loved you, and wanted to marry you. Hearing it again for the first time in a long while may distract him altogether from what you're doing.

I've never heard a single report of a case where the husband asked his wife what the heck was going on when she began surrendering. We are all surprised when they say nothing, even when we are being so good!

Despite a forgiving audience, you may feel like an actress at times, delivering lines that you're not sure about,

Prescription to boost your emotional well-being

Make a commitment to yourself to practice surrendering for six months before you tell your husband anything about it. Instead of confiding in him, find a girlfriend or two who will listen and support you in your process.

acting like you're not scared when you're terrified, and thanking him for things that don't seem to be enough. Remember that the more you act like you respect, trust and appreciate him, the more intimate the two of you will be. You'll begin to remember why you wanted to marry this man in the first place, and he'll go to new lengths to please and pamper you. So even if you fall somewhere short of Meryl Streep and Gwyneth Paltrow, do the very best acting job you can muster. Make sure that if the academy were watching, they'd nominate you for an Oscar because you were so convincing.

I'm sure you've done this kind of acting before. Think of the times you've received gifts you didn't like but acted appreciative in front of the giver. You did it to be polite and because you didn't want to hurt any one's feelings. Your husband deserves the same politeness.

THE SPIRITUAL CONNECTION

As you may have guessed by now, surrendering to your husband is a spiritual journey that is analogous to surrendering to a power greater than yourself. It's a way to practice trusting in, relying on, and connecting with your higher power. As you continue to act in faith that you will be taken care of, you are increasing your faith in a greater being. This results in a more harmonious existence with the universe because you are developing your ability to yield your will in situations in which you are powerless. Relinquishing the *illusion* that you have control over things you cannot control is the cornerstone of serenity and peace.

As an example, imagine you go to the beach and start barking orders at the ocean. You tell the waves to calm down and the water to move back. Of course, nothing would happen. You could then jump up and down and scream at the ocean to do as you say, but still nothing would change. By this time, you would probably be agitated

"It's great to work with somebody who wants to do things differently."

— *Keith Bellows*

and stressed out but no closer to getting the ocean to do what you tell it to do. By comparison, if you go to the beach and admire the incredible force and beauty of the waves without trying to alter them, you can just relax and enjoy yourself. This latter scenario can be nourishing and energizing, instead of depleting and frustrating. This is a simple metaphor for surrendering.

Perhaps you call your higher power God or Goddess, Buddha, or Allah. Maybe you call on Spirit, The Universe, or the Cosmic Teddy Bear in the Sky. Whatever your faith, make a decision to yield your will to your God and trust that your husband is God's instrument.

If you don't have a higher power or don't believe in one, surrendering to your husband is going to be a very tough leap. The underlying belief that your God is taking care of you throughout the surrendering process is a critical ingredient for success. Otherwise, you're putting all of your faith in another human being, who, however worthy, will eventually let you down. A surrendered wife believes that the God of her understanding is her source for all things. This helps her tap into the spiritual principles of detachment and acceptance in relationship to her husband.

It is possible to act as if you believe in a higher power even if you don't. This is called acting in faith, and I highly recommend it. When I first started my spiritual journey almost thirteen years ago, I had to act as if I believed there was a higher power when I really didn't know. I had rejected the God of my childhood as being too neglectful, punishing, and lacking in compassion. In retrospect, I was probably transferring qualities that I disliked in my parents on to this God. Nevertheless, I wasn't ready to take this guy back, so I had to find a new belief. I did it by writing about what I wanted in a higher power. If I can do it, so can you. As an example, here's what I believe to be true about my higher power:

Prescription to boost your spiritual connection

Write five paragraphs describing your higher power. Is he or she generous or measured? Spontaneous or meticulous? Gentle or strict? What other qualities do you find in your higher power? What affection does he or she have for you?

My higher power is a creative, humorous, compassionate Spirit that manifests in my life through other people and my own inner voice. I get plenty of generous gifts from Spirit including my wonderful husband, my beautiful home, the inspiration to write, and the friendship of incredible women. I choose my own path, and Spirit honors my decisions, even if they are not in my best interest. Sometimes I meet unpleasant consequences this way, but Spirit is always there to show me what to do next. Spirit knows my every sadness and comforts me when I cry.

I can hear Spirit best when I am very quiet and introspective. I have a hard time connecting with Spirit when I'm in fear of the future. When I relax and trust that Spirit is taking care of me, things seem to flow more easily, and I find more laughter and joy in my day. Spirit seems to encourage this.

I know that I'm very precious to Spirit, and this makes me feel safe. I thank Spirit as much as I can. I try to remember that Spirit has made this day, and so in my eyes it is wonderful.

MARCH TO YOUR OWN DRUMMER

Some will tell you that surrendering is sexist, unfeminist, and reverses what we've earned through liberation. Others will say that it's not healthy. Still others will just say that surrendering to your husband makes you a victim or too vulnerable. Of course, the whole idea of surrendering is to become vulnerable as a means to becoming more intimate.

Intimacy in a marriage is that magical, indescribable feeling of knowing that you are passionately and tenderly loved and that you love back with complete abandon. This primal and spiritual state perpetuates a healthy sex life, the willingness to hang in through hard times, a spark of excitement in what would otherwise be an ordinary day, and that

"If a man does not keep pace with his companions, perhaps it is because he hears a different drummer. Let him step to the music which he hears, however measured or far away."

— Henry David Thoreau

"At first, people refuse to believe that a strange new thing can be done, and then they begin to hope it can be done, then they see it can be done—then it is done and all the world wonders why it was not done centuries ago."

Frances Hodgson Burnett

enduring look of affection you sometimes see from couples who have been together for a very long time. You cannot have intimacy without tremendous personal risk of rejection, abandonment, or betrayal. The more you reveal and invest yourself, the greater the risk and the greater the connection.

So you must risk to have intimacy even though your survival instincts will scream at you that vulnerability is stupid, that surrendering is insanity. Other people may discourage you, too. They might tell you that you ought to know more about what's going on, that you're letting your husband down by not giving him advice. They might say he needs to respect you before you respect him and that marriage isn't all it's cracked up to be, so just get used to it. You won't have to look far for someone to tell you the whole surrendered wife thing is crazy, but it isn't.

It's not crazy to want romance and passion in your marriage. It's not crazy to want to feel respect for your life partner. It's not crazy to give up doing things that deplete your spirit and ask for help. It's not crazy to learn to relax and let your husband take care of you. It's not crazy to stop trying to control things you have no control over. It is scary, but it's not crazy. Don't let people who lack your courage tell you any differently.

The Myth of Equality in Marriage

I use the term equality to describe what I expect in the workplace. I want equal pay, equal opportunity, and equal treatment. However, I was never successful in realizing this concept in my marriage. I thought equality meant that my husband and I would discuss things together and come up with a decision that suits us both, but it never seemed to work that way.

Although we were discussing things, it wasn't equal. Instead, I was telling him how I thought things should be. When he didn't agree, I subtly or not-so-subtly criticized him. When he thought about things out loud, I'd let him know the minute he said something I didn't approve of, lest he decided to go further in that dreadful direction. I used this vague notion of equality to make sure I was in charge of things. I was even in charge of things that were not really my concern like who he should buy Christmas presents for, when he had time to paint the house, and when he should take the car in for service. This was *not* equality because I had veto power over everything. I was stressed out and overwhelmed, and he was defended and distant.

Here are some examples of conversations my husband and I had before I surrendered. See if you find any equality.

Example 1: Gift for a Friend

Him: I want to get a present for Steve.

Me: Why? He didn't get you a present last year!

Him: Uhhh...

Me: Don't spend more than $20 because we can't really afford it. Do you have to get him something?

Him: Well...

Me: How about if I bake some cookies and we give him those?

Him: Yeah, I guess so.

Me: Okay then, that's what we'll do.

Example 2: Painting the House

Me: Let's paint the house today.

Him: Today? I was going to read the paper and relax. I don't want to paint it today.

Me: If we don't paint it today, when are we going to paint it? It's supposed to start raining next week. You never want to paint the house! What do you think the neighbors think of this place? It looks awful out there.

Him: I'm not painting today.

Me: Why not?

Him: I told you, I'm planning to relax.

Me: I'll paint it by myself then!

Him: I'll help you do it later, just not today.

Me: You never want to do it!

Him: Arrrggghhhh HH!

Example 3: Car Maintenance

Him: I'm going to take the car in next week to get that noise checked out.

Me: Next week? What if it's something serious? If you don't take it in right away, it could get worse and cost us more money!

Him: That's why I'm going to take it in.

Me: Yes, but I think you should take it in right away. Why wait until next week?

Him: I'm not going to have time this week.
Me: You need to make time for things like that.
Him: Yeah, okay.
Me: So are you going to take it in?
Him: Yes! I said I'm going to take it in!
Me: Maybe I can take it in for you.
Him: Uhhhh. No, that's okay. I'll do it.
Me: Are you sure? That way, I can take it in tomorrow instead of waiting.
Him: We'll see.

Post-Surrendering

Today, if I were to have those same conversations with my husband, they'd go something like this:

Example 1: Gift for a Friend

Him: I want to get a present for Steve.
Me: Okay.

Since I'm not running the household finances, I don't need to worry about what we can afford. I have my money, so this purchase will not impact me. Also, I respect that my husband has friends he'd like to buy gifts for, instead of discounting them, as I would have before. Finally, it's not up to me to pick a present for his friend!

Example 2: Painting the House

Me: I wish the outside of our house looked better. I want new paint. What do you think?
Him: I think we should go to the paint store, buy some paint and start painting.

This is a real-life example. Notice that I just said what I wanted, not how it should happen. He could also have said, "Let's hire somebody to do it." Of course, he

"I should be very glad if it were possible for you to see in me something else than an idle man of the worst type."

— Vincent Van Gogh

could have also said, "I think we should wait until spring and then paint it." I would have gone along with it if he had.

Example 3: Car Maintenance

Him: I'm going to take the car in next week to get that noise checked out.

Me: Thank you for taking care of that.

Once again, I don't need to worry about what we can afford. I also believe my husband can handle maintaining the car without any input from me.

I still use the term equality to describe what I want in the workplace; however, I'm much more cautious about using it to describe an ideal for marriage. Deferring to my husband on things that aren't any of my business (our finances, his friends, his work) and telling him what I want has resulted in a far closer, more satisfying union for us.

ROUND PEGS AND MARTIANS

People sometimes ask me why the roles in a marriage can't be reversed. Why can't the husband defer to his wife and tell her what he wants? Perhaps they can be reversed; however, it did not work for me, and it wasn't working for the women I know who adopted the principles of surrendering in their marriage. I have some ideas about why that is, which I'll explain in a minute. Keep in mind, however, that I have no formal training in marriage counseling or psychology. I am not a social scientist, nor do I have all the answers. I only have my own experience, so take it for what it's worth. Compare it to your experience and see if it fits.

When John Gray's book *Men Are From Mars, Women are From Venus* became a huge best-seller, I felt

---

Prescription for reviving passion

Examine the conversations in your marriage for equality. Who is making most of the decisions? Who does most of the talking in your conversations? Do the decisions result from both parties having equal say?

strangely validated. The remarkable number of sales of this book was an indication that Gray's message resonated with many people as truth. Here was a vote from the collective consciousness of our society that men and women are indeed *different*. For years, so many of us had tried so hard to say that men and women were alike. I was relieved by Gray's gentle reminder that we are not.

If book sales are a measure of agreement, many of us agree that women are Venusians and men are Martians. Said another way, women are round pegs, and men are square pegs. Naturally then, women are more comfortable in round holes and men are more comfortable in square holes. When a woman embraces the feminine role in her marriage and the man embraces the masculine role, everyone is more comfortable. True, a square peg can go into a round hole, and vice versa, but we all know how that feels after a while.

Eastern philosophy describes the same concept using the words yin and yang. Yin is the spirit of the female and yang is the spirit of the male. These two concepts are represented by shapes that fit together perfectly and form a circle. Two yins would not fit together, nor would two yangs. Instead, the two different, complementary shapes form a perfect balance.

You might argue that the woman could bring masculine energy and the man could bring feminine energy to the relationship and the two could fit together beautifully. Again, I think this is a case of trying to make a round peg fit into a square hole. It may not be easy, but I think it's preferable for the round peg to live in a round hole and the square peg to live in the square hole. In other words, our genders are significant to our wants and needs. If we acknowledge that and act accordingly, everyone is going to be more comfortable and satisfied.

As I became more aware of this concept, I started to

"I love the idea of there being two sexes, don't you?"

— James Thurber

"Respect a man, he will do

the more."

— James Howell, 1659

see a trend that I had not recognized before. Just as I was seeing miraculous healing and connection in unions where the wife was surrendering, I also noticed increasing hostility and conflict in marriages where the wife was not surrendering. Some of the marriages in this latter group were troubled with affairs and even divorce. In my view, these couples could only stay in uncomfortable roles for so long and no longer.

My version of equality in a marriage, therefore, is recognizing that men and women are different and that they balance each other. In general, we have fundamental differences that make us better suited for certain roles and responsibilities. Women are designed to receive and are happiest when they let someone take care of them, connect with other women, and follow their intuition. Men are happiest when they take care of and protect their families while their wives respect and appreciate them for it.

Obviously, a woman *can* take care of and protect herself and her family. Of course, a man likes to be taken care of at times. I'm not suggesting these gender-specific roles are the only way to live, but I am saying that they will make everyone involved happier. These roles will vary somewhat from couple to couple, but there are some remarkable similarities. The point of this book is to describe these roles in such a way that you can implement them in your marriage and find out if they work for you.

How to Respect Your Husband

It may not seem like it at the moment, but your husband wants to shower you with things that you love. As long as he knows you respect his thinking, all you have to do is tell him what you want, as in "I want a cat" or "I want a vacation" or "I want a new house." Whenever he can, the husband of a surrendered wife will gladly respond to these requests because one of his foremost goals is to keep his wife happy.

Sometimes when a woman is disrespectful to her husband's thinking, he reacts with stinginess and disinterest. The wife then excuses herself from having to respect him because he's so stingy and disinterested. He then continues to feel disrespected and continues to withhold, and the two of them are locked in a permanent standoff.

Instead of torturing yourself like that, just take the first step–start respecting him! To do this, I suggest you memorize this phrase: "Whatever you think." Practice saying it over and over again because it's difficult to form those words when you really need them most.

Use this phrase in conversation with your husband whenever he tells you what he thinks. Taking this one step has far-reaching implications for your life. For instance, if he comes up with a nutty thought that he should change jobs, and this strikes terror in your heart, you say,

Prescription for clearing up bad moods

If you find yourself feeling disgusted with your husband, think of three things that you're grateful he does and then thank him for them. Next, tell him that he makes you very happy, whether you feel that way or not.

"Whatever you think." If he says he thinks the kids should learn how to ski, and this sounds dangerous to you, you say, "Whatever you think." If he says he thinks the two of you should go out to dinner, and you think you should save money and eat at home, you say, "Whatever you think." Even if you think what he's saying is lunacy, you respond by reminding him that you respect what he thinks.

Keep in mind that thinking is not action. We all think about many things that we don't do, and we all need the freedom to muse out loud about whatever it is we're thinking. As simple as it sounds, it's not always easy to let your husband think out loud without criticizing, laughing at, dismissing, or insulting him. Still, it helps the intimacy in your marriage when you respect his thinking. The phrase "whatever you think" is very helpful for doing this. Think of it as a way of recognizing your new consciousness. Every time you hear yourself say it, you can pat yourself on the back for being willing to raise your consciousness in this regard.

Of course, this phrase also implies your agreement which means you're going to end up agreeing with a lot of things that you never would have before. This will be very scary because you will then realize you are totally out of control. You may have the sensation of being in a freefall. Remember that you never *had* control over any one's actions but your own. You may have believed that you had control over your husband when you weren't respecting his thinking, but you really didn't.

Many of us harbor the illusion that when we reject disagreeable thoughts and ideas immediately, those thoughts are less likely to become actions with unpleasant consequences. We believe that we won't have to deal with the financial uncertainty of a job change if we tell him it's not a good idea. We think we won't have to be afraid for our children's safety if we dismiss his idea of teaching them to ski. We won't have to watch our husbands suffer and curse while repairing the plumbing themselves if we give them 'the look' that lets them know we don't think they can do it.

The problem is that when we discourage our husbands from doing things we don't want them to do, we also discourage their spirits. We discourage their ambition, sexuality, and pride. We also let them know that they are not responsible for taking any initiative at all because we wives already know what's best and have complete veto power. We let them know we don't respect them.

By contrast, if you respond to your husband's ideas with trust, he will feel a new level of responsibility. If he says he can fix the plumbing himself, and you tell him that you agree with whatever he thinks, he will feel the full weight of the task on his shoulders and probably even some fear. He may think a little more seriously about the task before deciding whether or not he wants to take it on.

Obviously, no one is going to agree with her husband all the time, and I'm not suggesting that a surrendered wife should never disagree with her husband. You should definitely disagree with him any time he thinks you should do something that would hurt your body or your spirit. When this happens, tell him that you can't do as he suggests. For instance, if he thinks you should stay out in the sun all day without sunscreen, or hike through poison oak, or carry something that's too heavy, tell him that you can't. You should also decline to do things that hurt your spirit. This will vary depending on the woman. For instance, if your husband thinks you should work and it would hurt your spirit to be away from your children to go to work, then don't do it. If your husband thinks you should be a full-time mom and it would hurt your spirit to quit your job

"There is only one corner of the universe you can be certain of improving, and that's your own self."

— Aldous Huxley

Prescription for increasing intimacy

To the best of your ability, listen to your husband without criticizing, making fun of, laughing at, dismissing or insulting him. Even if his thoughts terrify you, try to respond with trust by saying "whatever you think."

to be with your children full-time, then don't do that. This will vary depending on you. The more clear you are about what your spirit needs to thrive (movies, friends, hot baths, meditation, naps, time to work, solitude, manicures, creative expression, etc.), the easier it will be to determine when you must say no. For clarity in a given situation, ask yourself: "Will this hurt my body? Will my spirit be dampened?" If not, try to respect his ideas.

The more you respect your husband's thinking, the more powerful and masculine he will feel, and the more he will want to treasure the woman who makes him feel that way. For greatest intimacy and connection, agree with your husband's ideas as much as possible—even when it scares you.

If this sounds hard, that's because it is. Before you give up on it though, think how lonely and frustrated you've felt about having to do everything by yourself. Remember how many times you've wished he would just take some initiative and notice what needs to be done. It really is no fun to feel alone with the responsibilities of a family. So your choices are to take the lonely road of being responsible for everything or the terrifying path of respecting his thinking. Both are hard! However, along the path of respect, you will find peace, relief, joy, and passion that you will never find any other way.

But! But! But!

"But what if he says or does something really stupid, then what do I do?"

"But what if I completely disagree with him?"

"But what if I know I'm right and he's wrong?

If you're like me and lots of other wives, you probably have lots of objections to the idea of respecting your husband's thinking.

"What about my thinking?" you might argue.

"Doesn't my thinking count too?" Of course it does. What you think is very important in lots of situations where you decide things for yourself. However, in the context of a marriage of the spirits, in true partnership, you will both be happier if you follow your husband's thinking when deciding things together. When a wife respects her husband, he naturally responds with more confidence in himself and gratitude for his wife. This makes him treasure her more, and spend more time and effort memorizing the things that make her happy.

"Sometimes it is a great joy just to listen to someone we love talking."

— *Vincent McNabb*

Another benefit of surrendering to our husbands is a priority shift. It seems to make more room for gratitude in space that was once filled with concern for better parking spots, overdue bills, and unchanged light bulbs. This priority shift happened for Cathy after she asked me whether she should tell her husband she didn't like the way he had hung the welcome mat up to dry by putting nails in it. "Now there are holes in my welcome mat," she complained. "Are you saying I shouldn't even tell him my opinion about that?"

Since there's no respectful way to tell your husband that he did something you consider stupid, a surrendered wife would not tell her husband her opinion about the welcome mat. Instead, she would keep in mind, as Cathy did, that this is a man who works hard to support her, will bring her a glass of water in bed, plays with the baby, and makes her laugh. In the great scheme of things, a few holes in the welcome mat are not a big deal.

Collette was in a similar situation when her husband accidentally threw out one of her toddler's favorite toys. "I'm the one who has to pay for this with my son," she told me, "because my husband will be at work when the temper tantrum starts this afternoon. I'm so angry, I could just spit!"

This husband she was thinking of spitting on also

had some good qualities. He had agreed to raise their son in her faith and not his, and he got along well with her family. He also worked hard to make money so his wife could stay home with their son. After some contemplation, Collette realized it was not in her best interest to bring up the toy and instead vented to friends about his transgression.

Your husband will say things that sound silly to you, just as you have probably said many things that sound quite silly to him. He's human, and he deserves the space to think about things, concoct crazy schemes, and make mistakes. He may lose money. He may make you late. The kids might get bruises or scratches. He may make a mess, or lose his job or let the bills go so long that the water gets turned off. None of those situations is permanent, none of them is life-threatening, and all of them are part of being human. When you find yourself in one of them, try to remember to keep breathing, and remind yourself that this too shall pass.

When things go wrong as a result of your husband's decisions, he is learning. Next time, he'll probably invest more carefully or have the kids wear kneepads or start on a beginner ski run. If you don't make a big deal about his mistakes, he'll begin to show more initiative in every area. Isn't that what you've always wanted? Somebody who had his own ideas and acted on them?

Beth had been surrendering for several months when the phone was disconnected for non-payment. She was scared and embarrassed about having to go to a neighbor's to call her husband at work. Instead of berating him or criticizing him for letting it happen, she simply told him the phone was shut off and that she did not like it. Before the day was through, her phone was back on, and Beth had had a chance to talk to other women about how scared she had been. When her husband came home from work, she thanked him for taking care of everything and resisted the temptation to rage at him.

"Men are born to succeed, not to fail."

— *Henry David Thoreau*

Perhaps Beth would have been justified in yelling at her husband and telling him it was unacceptable to have the phone shut off. She could have complained about the inconvenience and made ultimatums. That might even have made her feel better in the short run. Instead, she decided to stay in gratitude for her husband. As a result, the disconnection was a small inconvenience instead of a major trauma. Beth and her husband were able to maintain the intimacy and closeness they were accustomed to since she had surrendered.

"Silence is one of the hardest arguments to refute."

— Josh Billings

The following month, the electricity at *my* house was disconnected for non-payment. I thought of Beth and took inspiration from her serenity around having a utility disconnected. I actually laughed out loud at the irony. Here I was, writing a book telling other women to trust their husbands to pay the bills, and in the process of doing just that, our electricity was shut off!

This particular day I was not writing under deadline for a client. Instead, I was leisurely writing this book. The weather happened to be gorgeous, and I wish I could tell you that I took this opportunity to go out in the backyard and enjoy the sun. I wish I could say that we ate dinner out and lit candles that evening. I wish I could say I had the serenity to let my husband take care of everything. Unfortunately, I can't tell you that without lying like a rug.

Instead of relaxing, I went into survival mode, located the checkbook, and went to the nearest payment office. I wrote a check to the electric company even though I had no idea what was in our checking account. The power was back on in a couple of hours, but I had missed an opportunity to trust and relax.

When I called Beth to tell her she was not the only one who had had this experience, I realized that I would probably have to live through the whole episode again, just so I could get it right the next time. Perhaps I will, but I hope not. In any case, I'm clear that I would survive the experience and maybe even have a good laugh about it.

AVOID BANGING YOUR HEAD AGAINST THE WALL

Another common form of masochism that I used to engage in with my husband was trying to get him to do something I wanted him to do. It never worked for me, and I've noticed it didn't work for other wives I know either. Instead, my husband and I would end up in a mother/son role with me trying to cajole, encourage, convince, and bribe him into completing a certain task. Meanwhile, he would resist the task as mightily as he could until both of us were worn down and frustrated.

"When a man points a finger at someone else, he should remember that four of his fingers are pointing at himself."

— Louis Nizer

To avoid banging your head against the wall, don't ask your husband to do things that you want him to do. This includes asking him to clean the attic, take out the trash, and bathe the kids. Instead, be grateful for the things he does of his own accord. Thank him profusely to reward behavior that you want to encourage, but don't make demands on him.

Gabriella and Scott struggled with this constantly before she surrendered. She complained that he would never do anything if she didn't tell him to. She told me he didn't even seem to notice things that needed to be done! Still, she was tired of asking, so she decided to refrain from making demands.

That evening, when Scott came home from work, she did not ask him to bathe the kids as she normally did. Instead, they talked about the day and watched some television. Finally, Scott turned to her and said, "Are we going to bathe the kids or what?" She smiled at him and said, "Good idea!"

As Gabriella learned, Scott was quite aware of what needed to be done and was even willing to do it. He just didn't want to be told what to do. This is a really important point because it's such a big temptation to ask your husband to do things. For the sake of your poor aching head, stop banging it against a wall. Don't ask him to do things you want him to do.

THE ROMANTIC APPROACH

Let's suppose you want more romance in your marriage. Let's suppose further that your husband is gone a lot because he works too much or plays golf frequently. You might feel that if he would just work or golf a little less and stay home a little more, you would get more attention. In your mind, whatever is taking all his time is preventing you from having more candlelight dinners and bubble baths for two. You might begin to resent whatever he does while he's away because, in your mind, you are in competition with that activity for his time and attention.

Megan felt this way about her husband's job, and so she often told him she was sick of him working so much and that she needed help around the house. When this didn't have the desired effect of keeping him home more, she *demanded* that he spend more time at home, adding that she couldn't do everything by herself. Megan's husband still didn't change his habits, however, and she found herself more alone than ever. Even worse, she felt unloved and resentful because her husband seemed to have no regard for what she wanted.

Megan's husband was probably feeling pretty defensive and unappreciated about the whole thing. I've heard men say things like: "Doesn't she realize that the reason I work so hard is for her?" Further, Megan's requests probably sounded like pressure to her husband who was trying to balance the needs of his job with the needs of his family. Finally, there was nothing inviting about her appeal to come home to do more work. He probably figured he had enough work to do at his job without coming home early to do

"Success in life consists of going from one mistake to the next without losing enthusiasm."

— Winston Churchill

some more.

  After surrendering, Megan learned that beneath her feelings of anger and overwhelm was a more vulnerable feeling: loneliness. She missed her husband when he was gone a lot. She was lonely for him. Through the process of surrendering, she learned to say to her husband, "I miss you" instead of trying to control or nag him into doing what she wanted.

  As you can imagine, this approach seemed more inviting to her husband who managed to leave work earlier twice that week. As Megan continued to practice being vulnerable by expressing how much she missed him, she noticed that the romance in her marriage seemed more alive than ever. Through this process, she had an important realization: Romance is not something that your husband does or doesn't do for you. Instead, Megan learned that she could cultivate romance in her relationship by being romantic herself. In each moment, all of us make the choice to express our honest feelings in a way that is romantic or in a way that stifles romance.

  Saying "I miss you" instead of "I'm sick of you never being home" is one example. This lets your mate know that he is more than a packhorse who can lift heavy things for you. It tells him that you enjoy his company. Far more important than candles and bubble baths, a tender tone can help create romance in your marriage.

  Some women object to telling their husbands they miss them because they say that's not how they feel. "I'm just overwhelmed taking care of the kids by myself all the time," they tell me. The truth is these women do miss something about their husbands. Whether you miss his help or his presence as a disciplinarian or your lover's touch is immaterial. Your honest message is the same. You miss him! As with the other "mantras" of a surrendered wife, saying "I miss you" is far more vulnerable than telling your

Prescription for wives who want to see their husbands more

The next time you find yourself wishing your husband wouldn't read, watch T.V., work, golf or tinker so much, tell him you miss him. Say it as often as you feel it, even if you feel silly saying it, and let go of the results.

husband to get his butt home.

Once again, it will take more courage to deliver this fragile message than it does to nag, cajole, or criticize. If you crave romance, I assure you this is a worthwhile risk. When Melissa first told her husband that she missed him, he did not change his behavior at all initially. Still, she continued to tell him this when she felt it. A few weeks later, he called to say he was leaving a business trip early and driving in traffic to come home right away. "I miss you," he told her, echoing what she had been saying for the past few weeks.

Another way to promote romance in your marriage is to listen carefully for *heart messages*. A heart message is what's hidden underneath words that sound like a call to battle. For instance, when my husband got a higher-paying job recently, he made a sarcastic comment that he hoped he was making enough money for me. I felt surprised and hurt by this, but I didn't react. A few minutes later, I took this opportunity to tell him I was proud of him for getting this new job and that I felt well taken care of and happy with him. He perked up immediately, and I haven't heard a comment like that from him since.

I was lucky that time because I was able to sort through the words and tone in his message to hear the heart message—that he wanted some reassurance and appreciation. More often than not, I don't even realize there's a message beneath the message until I talk to someone else about it. Around here, heart messages are sometimes hidden under what sounds like a complaint. The romantic approach is to respond to these complaints by addressing the real message.

Here are some examples of comments that have hidden heart messages:

Message: "Stop giving those kids everything they want!"

"When nobody around you seems to measure up, it's time to check your yardstick."

— Bill Lemley

Heart Message: I want you to pay attention to me.

Message: "No matter what I do around here, it's never enough for you!"
Heart Message: I hope you appreciate me. I want you to notice what I do.

Message: "There's no pleasing you, is there?"
Heart Message: I'm afraid I don't make you happy. I hope I'm adequate as a husband.

Prescription for reducing stress

Think of a problem that you're challenged with that you could use some help with. Ask your husband what he thinks you should do about it, and then be prepared to take the action (or inaction) he suggests.

As you can see, heart messages are difficult to hear and require some careful listening. I've found that the connection that results is worth the effort.

WILL THE REAL VICTIM PLEASE STAND UP?

The scariest part about surrendering to your husband is that, between relinquishing the finances and respecting his thinking, it seems like you're never going to get to express your opinion, much less get your own way. Some women object to this because they don't want to be victims. What they don't realize is that surrendering actually shifts them into a position of *power*. To illustrate this elusive concept, consider the hypothetical cases of Wilma and Erma.

Wilma is overwhelmed with doing everything around the house, going to work, taking care of the kids, and trying to make ends meet when she pays the bills. She has to nag her husband to get him to do things for her, but when he forgets, she frequently ends up doing them herself. Wilma tells her husband her opinion about how everything should be done, but he can never seem to get it right. Although Wilma doesn't realize it, he is on the verge of having an affair with a co-worker who admires him.

Erma's also busy taking care of kids, but her husband earns most of the income and pays all of the bills for the family, so she doesn't worry about that. She often asks her husband for help and relinquishes tasks that are stressful for her such as parent-teacher conferences for their son. Erma rarely tells her husband what to do, but he is always thinking of things to please her. Although Erma doesn't realize it, her husband is shopping for a diamond anniversary ring for her.

Wilma is staying in control of everything to avoid being a victim. Erma is relinquishing control to her husband so she can relax more. Which one do you think has the most power? Which one would you rather be?

LET HIM SOLVE YOUR PROBLEMS

Prior to surrendering, I used to ask my husband's opinion about things then dismiss whatever he said in favor of my own ideas. This used to irritate him to no end. What I was actually doing was trying to get him to give me the *right* answer which, of course, would be the same as what I thought. Every time he said something that I disagreed with, it fortified my belief that he wasn't really somebody I could depend on. I probably should have just married myself and saved us both a lot of trouble!

Today, I not only listen to my husband's ideas, I make a point of following his suggestions whenever I can. For instance, my husband was the one who thought of the idea of registering the domain name *surrenderedwife.com* so that I could host a website on the Internet to help other women learn about surrendering. When he first made this suggestion, it didn't sound all that important to me, but I went along with it. Later, after *The Los Angeles Times* had come to interview me for an article about our Surrendered Circle and the philosophy of The Surrendered Wife, I started to feel stressed out about having hundreds of women call me for more information. I wanted to help as many women as I could, but I also knew I could only take so

"The supreme happiness of life is the conviction that we are loved."

— *Victor Hugo*

"It's better to ask some of

the questions than to have

all the answers."

— James Thurber

many phone calls a day. I asked my husband what he thought I should do, and he said, "I think we should build a website and ask the *Times* to refer to it in the article. That way, anyone who wants the information can get it online."

Suddenly, his idea of registering the domain name made sense to me. Building a website on the Internet was a perfect way to share the information about surrendering without depleting our resources. I might not have thought of it on my own, so my husband thought of it for me. All I had to do was follow his direction.

I don't ask my husband to solve all of my problems, of course. Many of the challenges I come up against I can and do handle myself. At times when I'm stuck, however, I've found that he's a tremendous resource for helping me come up with solutions. I just had never learned to take advantage of his help until I surrendered.

Many of us who had been so controlling had a hard time making this transition. We were so used to taking care of everything by ourselves that it just didn't occur to us to ask our husbands what they thought about our problems. For instance, my friend Phoebe called me one day because she was frustrated with her two-year-old and she needed some input. I listened and was able to sympathize with her plight but, when push comes to shove, I don't have any experience raising a child. I didn't have any advice or solutions to offer her, but I reminded her that her husband probably did. She asked him for help that evening, and he made a simple suggestion that was very effective and helpful. This reminded Phoebe that she wasn't alone raising her children. She remembered why she admired her husband in the first place.

Keep in mind that a respectful wife follows her husband's advice whenever she can. That means you can't ask him for input and then ignore what he says because that's not what you think. If you're going to ask, be prepared to go along with his response. That doesn't mean that you can't have a dialog about it—just don't try to argue your thinking against his. Instead, stick to telling him how you feel and what you want. Keep in mind that your husband's thinking is influenced by how you feel, just as his thinking will also color how you feel. If he thinks you should have a teacher conference on your child's behalf and you don't want to, you can say so. If he still thinks you should, then go ahead. He may change his mind once he hears what you want, so don't be afraid to share your feelings. His first reaction is not necessarily his best thinking, so let the conversation run its course.

Deferring to what my husband thought was the part of surrendering that I had the most resistance to. I know that I'm smart and I didn't see why my husband's thinking should be more important than mine. I spent some time hating the whole idea of doing what he thought was right when I disagreed. Then, as I started to rely on his thinking more, I began to feel truly relieved knowing that I could get his help and that I wasn't alone. I came to see this new arrangement as a form of negotiation that felt better than steamrollering over him. Now I even keep lists of things I want to ask his opinion about. This is yet another aspect of intimacy that's been restored to our marriage as part of surrendering.

"Being nice should never be perceived as being weak. It's not a sign of weakness, it's a sign of courtesy, manners, grace, a woman's ability to make everyone... feel at home, and it should never be construed as weakness."

— Benazier Bhutto, Prime Minister of Pakistan

Financial Suicide and Other Marital Adventures

CHAPTER

6

Along with sex and parenting, money is one of the most common subjects that married couples argue about. Having tried a variety of approaches to managing household finances in our marriage, I can certainly see why. As a controlling wife, all of my approaches included retaining some degree of control over our household expenditures. If you are like me in this area, one of the most important steps you can take towards finding peace and true intimacy in your marriage is relinquishing control of the household finances as described in this chapter.

For me, the steps outlined below seemed like financial suicide. Yet as I have continued on this path, I have found myself feeling more prosperous, more treasured, and far more relaxed. This process was the death of an unhealthy habit of obsessing about money and trying to control my husband's spending and earning, and the birth of a new intimacy with my husband. As with the other practices of a surrendered wife, this new approach to finances is just as terrifying as it is gratifying.

Because you are reading this book, it's pretty likely that you are primarily responsible for paying the bills in your household. However, if your husband already handles the household finances congratulations for having already

"The greater part of our happiness or misery depends on our dispositions, and not on our circumstances. We carry the seeds of the one or the other about with us in our minds wherever we go."

— Martha Washington

embarked on this difficult journey. I applaud your faith and ability to trust. You are already enjoying a degree of intimacy that many women have never experienced. You are off to a good start, but I still encourage you to read this chapter both for a glimpse at what goes on in other relationships and to check for ways that you might still be subversively controlling with money.

If you are responsible for all or part of the finances in your union, please read this entire chapter carefully before you take any steps towards relinquishing the household bills to your husband. If you follow the guidelines laid out here, you'll be able to avoid some common pitfalls.

Please, do not mistake these suggestions as expert tax preparation, investment, or estate planning tips. I am not a financial expert. My purpose in making these suggestions is to share practices that have been effective for me and for other women in becoming more intimate with our husbands. My evidence is strictly anecdotal and unscientific; however, as a pleasant side-effect, I've noticed many couples seem to enjoy greater prosperity after the wife surrenders the finances to her husband.

If you've long suspected that your husband could be making more money or doing more with his talents, you're probably right. In the past, he's had to spend a good portion of his energy defending himself against you. However, once he feels respected at home, two things happen: the energy that was formerly diverted to defending himself is freed up for other things and his self-esteem increases. If the woman who knows him best in the whole world thinks he's smart and capable then he will start to believe that he is indeed pretty sharp.

Along with these improved feelings of worth, I often see an increase in income. It makes sense if you think about it. The more you feel you're worth, the more likely you are to prosper. For instance:

- Theresa's husband Steve got a $20,000-a-year raise just a few months after Theresa adopted the principles of a surrendered wife.
- Gina has no idea how much money her husband is making now, but she has a lot more disposable income than she did before she started surrendering.
- Karen and her family moved from their two-bedroom rental into their own four-bedroom, two-bath house shortly after she surrendered.

STEP 1: MERGE YOUR MONEY

There can be no intimacy unless there is vulnerability, and one of the ways wives avoid vulnerability (and therefore intimacy) is with money. As an act of your faith in your husband's ability to earn, spend, and manage money wisely, give him all of the money you receive from other sources. At the same time, give him a list of your planned expenditures for the next month (this is covered in detail in Step 2), so he can provide you with the money you need.

"There is no wealth but life."

— John Ruskin

If reading this paragraph makes your heart beat faster and your breathing shallow, join the club. Your mind may be racing with objections to this suggestion. After all, without even trying, you could find a legion of feminists, accountants, financial advisors, and marriage counselors who would say giving your husband all your money and asking for what you need in return is a bad idea. Yet, I've often witnessed this process bringing peace and happiness to couples who employ it. In fact, I've never seen it fail to make both husband and wife happier.

As with other aspects of surrendering to your husband, this is not a good idea for women whose have an active addiction, such as alcoholism or gambling, or whose husbands are physically abusive. If your husband does not fall into one of these categories, then I highly recommend that you at least give this a try. Even if you make more money. Even if you've maintained separate accounts for years and it's working just fine. Even, and especially, if you don't trust him not to bounce checks or spend unwisely. Even if you think you'll have less money for yourself. Keep in mind that you can always go back to the way you're doing things now. Act as if you have every confidence that your husband can handle this, and then brace yourself for the abundance and prosperity that will follow.

"Money doesn't buy happiness. The fellow with $50 million is no happier than the fellow with $40 million."

— Anonymous

STEP 2: MAKE A SPENDING PLAN

Make a spending plan that lists only the things you need to buy yourself. For instance, my spending plan includes funds for clothes, makeup, gas for my car, going out with my girlfriends, facials and manicures, books, CDs, massage, groceries and home furnishings like throw pillows and linens. That's about it. My spending plan does not include things such as my car payment, the cleaning lady or my student loans. My husband pays those directly. My friends who have children also cover their children's needs in their spending plans, including toys, diapers, clothes, baby-sitting, entertainment, etc.

The spending plan you submit to your husband should be itemized with an accounting of how much you want to spend on everything. As an example, here's mine for a typical month:

new towels:	$50
groceries:	$350
new dress and shoes:	$100
cleaners:	$25
gas:	$40

car wash:	$15
haircut:	$52
manicures:	$36
facial:	$50
prescriptions:	$20
eating out with friends:	$40
CDs/ books:	$30
volleyball class:	$20
gift:	$40
TOTAL	$868

Before you submit your spending plan to your husband, call a girlfriend, or even two, and double check it with them to make sure it sounds generous enough to live on. When in doubt, ask for a little more because you don't want to have to go back to him in the middle of the month and ask for more money for groceries.

Don't worry that your husband may not be able to afford your spending plan. This is not your concern. When you give it to him, it will be up to him to decide if you get all of it or not. Perhaps you will get more, perhaps you will get less. In either case, you should thank him for the money and make do with it.

Your spending plan should NOT include household expenses such as rent or mortgage, utilities, credit card bills, car payments or other fixed monthly expenses. Don't include the cost of going out on a date with your husband as that will be his responsibility. You will not need to worry about any of that because you are about to take the next terrifying step.

"When a fellow says, 'it ain't the money but the principle o' the thing,' it's the money."

— Abe Martin

STEP 3: RELINQUISH CONTROL OF THE FINANCES TO YOUR HUSBAND

Proceed with caution on this step as it's a bit tricky. I've seen some wives who are ostensibly surrenderring the finances to their husband approach it by saying, "You have to take care of the checkbook and give me money for my spending plan." Unfortunately, this is still telling him what to do and does not improve things at all.

Instead, you'll want to approach this with a spirit of humility by telling your husband that you are relinquishing control of the household finances because you can't do it anymore. The truth is, you can't do it *and* expect to have the kind of intimacy with your husband that you desire.

One wife asked me if there should be a training period for showing her husband how to balance the checkbook since she had been doing it so long. If your husband is a grown man, and most husbands are, this is not necessary. Instead, explain that you need help, it's making you crazy, and you feel he could do a better job with managing the money. That's all you need to say, so once you've said it, STOP TALKING. And brace yourself. Do not explain how to balance the checkbook. Do not tell him which bills need to be paid. Do not offer any assistance at all unless he specifically asks you for help.

After I had a discussion about this with Lynda, she asked her husband if he wanted to take the checkbook. Of course, he said "No, that's okay." Then Lynda called me to tell me that she couldn't do this because her husband didn't want to. This came as no surprise to me because Lynda had not relinquished control. Instead, she had asked for permission to keep control, and gotten it.

If you've been mommying your husband for any length of time, this will not be an easy conversation because he will not like this idea one bit. In my experience,

Prescription for increasing your prosperity

Once you've completed this chapter, go back to the beginning and take each of the steps. For best results, follow the instructions carefully. If you're thinking you'll surrender in every way except for financially, think again.

the husband tends to put up a fight of some kind. That's exactly what happened when Liz tried to relinquish the household finances to her husband. Gregg acted angry and disappointed in her. "I thought we were a team," he complained. "I don't have time to do it because I work so much. It's easier for you to do it than it is for me."

Fortunately, Liz was able to resist this bait and say nothing. Gregg did take over the checkbook, and later he even took over the books for Liz's business. The last time I talked to Gregg, he said he wouldn't give up control of the finances at his house for anything. Instead, he was feeling powerful and accomplished at providing so well for his family. Of course, that was partly because Liz had done such a good job with the next step.

"There is no security in this life. There is only opportunity."

— Douglas MacArthur

STEP 4: STICKING TO YOUR SPENDING PLAN

The word budget, like the word diet, implies restriction. It brings to mind clipping coupons or having to eat tuna fish for weeks on end. In contrast, a spending plan allows us to live comfortably and well. You may even set out to spend more than you normally do in your spending plan. However you do it, be sure that you *stick* to your spending plan.

Sticking to your spending plan is important because it helps your husband predict expenses. You let him know that you will be taken care of for the month or the week if he gives you the amount you ask for. If you come back in the middle of the month or the week with no money left, you have now broken the original agreement and become a bottomless pit of expense. A restrictive spending plan is a setup for failure, so be generous to yourself in your plan especially for the first month.

This is not a good time to quit long-standing habits in order to save money and reduce your spending. For instance, if you buy a cup of coffee every morning and you're thinking you could save money by having a cup at home instead, don't leave it out of your spending plan. For now, just indulge yourself, and be sure to let your husband know how grateful you are for that fresh coffee every morning.

Tell your husband you want your spending plan money in cash. He can give you a certain amount weekly, monthly, or on paydays. There are several benefits to doing this. One is that you'll never need to use a credit card, ATM card, or checkbook to pay for anything. Without those so-called "conveniences," it's harder to spend more than you have and easier to figure out what the heck happened on the monthly statement. It's also a very rich feeling to have all that money in your purse. If you're not comfortable carrying that much cash, you can always take just what you need and leave the rest at home.

Having cash in your purse also gives you autonomy to spend what you want when you want, instead of having to find out if there's money in the checking first. It gives you the assurance that all your financial needs will be met which tends to reduce the need to impulse shop. Just as you will tend to drink only what you need when water is readily available, you will spend only what you need when money is readily available. If either water or money is in short supply, you may feel inclined to consume as much as possible while you have the chance. Therefore, having an ample supply contributes to healthy spending.

If you find you really have trouble sticking to your spending plan, you may be a compulsive spender. In this case, I highly recommend you contact a group called Debtors Anonymous, or DA for short. DA is patterned after Alcoholics Anonymous and provides a spiritual program to help compulsive debtors and spenders learn to make good decisions with money. If you continue to spend or debt

"Money isn't everything,

as long as you have

enough."

— *Malcolm Forbes*

compulsively, there is little hope of having true intimacy with your husband. Since DA is a free program, there's no reason not to contact them now:

Debtors Anonymous
P.O. Box 920888, Needham, MA 02492-0009
phone: 781-453-2743
website: www.debtorsanonymous.org

STEP 5: TRUST YOUR HUSBAND

Letting your husband handle the bills and give you a cash allowance frees you from having to worry about a number of annoying things like balancing the checkbook, running to the ATM machine, and figuring out whether or not you can afford to go out to dinner. Knowing that you don't have to pay the bill at a restaurant will free you to admire and converse with your husband instead of thinking about how he could have ordered the spaghetti instead of the veal to save money. I call this transformation the miracle of perpetual dating.

Perpetual dating literally means returning to the roles each of you played during your courtship. Remember how much fun that was? Let him open the door for you. Order what appeals to you instead of trying to keep the price down. Don't begrudge him spending money on his soda. Thank him for dinner, and tell him how much you enjoyed being with him. Let him take you out the way he used to. In my experience, both husband and wife end up liking this arrangement very much, but everybody has a hard time getting started with it.

In fact, each and every wife I've suggested these five steps to has had a list of objections as long as my arm. Some wives are concerned that managing the household finances will be too much of a burden for a husband who is busy, or works so hard, or has health problems, or is not

"One does not toss out the gold because the bag is dirty."

— Buddha

good at math. Whatever your objection, what you are saying is that your husband is incapable. Mostly, you are probably afraid to rely on him.

Have a little faith. If it feels like you're jumping off a cliff, in a way, you are. On the other hand, what choice do you have? You've tried doing things your way, and you're not happy—at least not as happy as you think you could be. Plus, you're exhausted from having to do everything. You've come this far, so you might as well put on your seat belt and stay for the ride.

Trusting your husband means you don't open the mail to see if he paid the bills on time. It means you don't check the balance in the checking account to see what's in there. It means you don't panic when he makes a mistake that costs him money. As long as your needs are met—if there's a roof over your head, gas in your car, food in your refrigerator, money in your purse—try not to panic. It's quite possible that you're married to a mere mortal man who will not do things perfectly but who wants to take care of you and make you happy. Give him a chance to do that.

Some wives were concerned that their husbands were stingy and wouldn't let them have any of life's luxuries. Stingy husbands are a common by-product of controlling wives, and in every case I've seen, the stinginess leaves when the wife relinquishes control. You won't know if your husband is generous or not until you let go of the finances in your home. For a preview of coming attractions, think about whether you found him stingy during your courtship. The man who wooed you is about to return...if you'll let him.

"I had plastic surgery last week. I cut up my credit cards."

— Henny Youngman

Reruns of Father Knows Best

If Carolyn's husband Kevin was nervous about taking care of three toddlers, including their two-year-old daughter, for the day, he didn't show it. During his watch, one of the boys got diarrhea that ran down the legs of his overalls and threatened to make a huge mess. Kevin quickly took the boy out in the back yard to hose him off in the warm July sun. The boy seemed to enjoy this, and it took care of the mess. Still, Carolyn and the boy's mother were surprised that a grown man wouldn't think to use the bathtub.

Jean was just as surprised when she came home late one Saturday morning to find her two boys still in their pajamas watching cartoons. Although their father had been supervising, an empty box of cookies was the only evidence that they had eaten breakfast that morning.

The moral of these stories is that fathers do not do things the same way mothers do. Sometimes mothers are shocked and horrified at this, but the truth is children have a mother and a father for a reason. Just because a father does things differently doesn't mean he's doing them wrong. A woman only knows how to be a good mother. Only a man knows how to be a good father. Therefore, any time a woman tries to tell a man how to be a good father,

Prescription to help you relax

Make a list of the things your husband does differently from you as a parent. How are his methods better? (We already know you think your methods are better, but just go along with this exercise.)

she is way out of line. She has no idea!

On the other hand, since I don't have children, I really have no idea how to be a parent. *I* would be way out of line telling you how to do it, particularly if you've got more on-the-job training than me. Instead, I will just report on what I have witnessed in the relationships where I have been privileged to watch the family dynamics before and after the wife begins to surrender.

For instance, before Candace started surrendering to her husband Joel, raising their two boys was a point of contention. Candace's list of grievances about her husband included playing too rough with the boys, letting them watch too much television, and spending too little time with them. She disapproved of him wrestling with them constantly, so she urged him to be gentler with her precious babies. After she began to surrender, she quickly realized that interfering in her husband's relationship with his own children wasn't helping anyone. Candace was unnecessarily stressed and worried; Joel was grumpy when he felt criticized as a parent; and the two boys were missing out on learning how to be men. From my observations, wrestling appears to be a chief activity for the healthy, developing man-child in our species. Today, Joel is just as much a parent to the boys as Candace is, and his instincts for how to raise them are just as valid and important in their family.

Before Tina surrendered to her husband Gregg, their three daughters were more likely to ask Tina for help than their father, mostly because they recognized her as the authority around the house. As the girls observed Tina treating their father with more respect, however, they began to follow suit.

One day their 13-year-old daughter Brittany was flipping through a magazine and came across a quiz called "Is Your Husband A Grown-Up?" When Brittany started asking Tina the questions in regards to Gregg's grown-up-ness, Tina stopped her and told her that of course daddy was a grown-up. She added that the article was inappropriate and disrespectful.

Later that night, Brittany thanked her dad at the dinner table for working so hard to support all of them. Tina knew they had turned a corner especially when she noticed the girls asking their father for what they needed more frequently. This relieved Tina from the pressure of feeling like the only parent. Now there were clearly two, and she had someone else to defer to when she needed help.

Prior to surrendering, both Tina and Candace had concerns that their husbands were neglectful to the children. In reality, their husbands were defensive and withdrawn out of self-preservation. This is not to say that the mother is responsible if the father has a poor relationship with his children. She is not. However, a man who feels respected and accomplished is far more likely to show up as a good father than one who feels criticized and defeated. Just like the old television show "Father Knows Best," your husband does know better than you do how to be the dad. It's in your best interest, as well as your children's, to leave that department to him.

I have noticed that men show up for their roles as fathers in a completely different way once they feel respected by their wives. As a result of watching other families, I've come to believe that even in cases where a man is verbally abusive to his children, there is much hope of the family being restored. Children are less likely to be punished inappropriately, and more likely to be attended to generously when their father feels respected by his wife.

Some women have found a whole new perspective on "inappropriate" punishment, as in Lucy's case. Lucy felt that her husband's idea of crime and punishment was too

"Ward, could you talk to the Beaver?"

— June Cleaver

"There can be no defense

like elaborate courtesy."

— *E.V. Lucas*

harsh. She made sure to tell her husband this and negotiated for leniency on her son's behalf. Ironically, the boy was not responding to her discipline as she had hoped. She felt frustrated because he was repeating the same undesirable behavior over and over again. Finally, she understood that while she had been trying to protect him, she was doing her son a disservice by saving him from his own consequences.

So what does it look like to surrender to a man in regard to his fathering? The same rules apply to surrendering in general; don't criticize, don't offer advice, don't correct or instruct. In addition, make a point of referring your children to your husband for permission or help, particularly if you're the parent who spends the majority of the time with the kids. For instance, if the family is at a store and your child approaches you and asks if he can have something, you could refer him to dad by saying, "Whatever your father thinks." If dad says no, the answer is no. Contradicting your husband's decision undermines his authority, so to be respectful you must agree in both words and actions.

Kelly had a hard time doing this when she and her husband Jerry took their son to an amusement park. In the past, she had taken their son to the park without Jerry and had made a ritual of buying the boy a lollipop when they were there. In an effort to start relinquishing some control, she asked Jerry if he thought their son should have a lollipop, and he said no. Kelly was sure he was being too harsh and was terribly unhappy with this response. She bit her tongue anyway in an effort to respect his decision. That day, their son had no lollipop.

The next time they went to the amusement park, Kelly had been respecting Jerry for some time, and everyone in the family was enjoying the new harmony and closeness. This time, Jerry was happy to buy a lollipop for his little boy. The time after that, he came up with the idea of buying a lollipop with no prompting.

Naturally, Kelly had an easier time respecting Jerry when he was being generous with lollipops, but they may have never gotten to that point if she hadn't been willing to uphold his decision when he said no. You also must be willing to respect your husband's difficult decisions in order to get to the other side. Even if you think your child is suffering unnecessarily. Even if you're sure your husband is wrong or too strict or pigheaded. Unless he is physically abusing the children, do your best not to interfere. Again, you are setting up a positive expectation for your husband to be a good father, and only he knows about that.

There is a significant difference between physical restraint and physical abuse. I have seen cases where the father used physical restraint to discipline or control a child and the mother was horrified. Although I'm not an advocate for this particular technique in child-rearing, your husband's decision to use physical restraint is *not* good justification for leaving him or treating him disrespectfully. Again, all parents are imperfect. If you are struggling to have compassion for your husband's mistakes when it comes to the kids, think about all the times you've done things you wished you hadn't with your children. Now imagine he had threatened to leave you and take the kids each time you made those mistakes.

Your husband may test you in this area consciously or unconsciously. He may purposely do something he knows you have always disapproved of in order to test the limits of your respect. You won't always pass the test, but at least now you know when you're walking into quicksand. It won't be long before you learn to navigate around it entirely.

"I often regret that I have spoken; never that I am silent."

— Publilius Syrus

WHAT DADDY SAYS, GOES

It's not right, it's not fair, and it's not justifiable, but couples sometimes use kids as battering rams when there's conflict in the marriage. If, for instance, the husband thinks his wife is undermining his authority with the kids by contradicting him or ignoring him, he may inappropriately take out some anger and frustration on the kids. This situation will be intensified if the husband is feeling jealous that the little people in the house get all your attention and affection. This situation gets ugly real fast.

So what are your options? As always you can only control *your* actions, not his. For instance, if you tell him he's inappropriately angry with the kids, he'll probably become even more defensive and obnoxious, or, at best, he'll tune you out. In addition, you will feel the unpleasant and unnecessary stress of trying to control something you have no control over. I have never seen a woman get what she wants by trying to correct her husband, but I have seen her exacerbate the situation this way.

Another option is to recognize that you are powerless over how your husband treats your children and say nothing at all. This will be tough at first, but in the long run it will relieve you of unnecessary stress. Also, in this case, since no one is yelling at him to behave differently, he will probably feel the full impact of his own guilt if he has been inappropriate with the kids. This will weigh more heavily on him than your criticism.

Still another option is to look for ways that you can improve your relationship with your husband. Recognize that you may have put him in a difficult situation by undermining his authority. It may seem like it's all his fault, but if by some chance you have been disrespectful, apologize for it to reclaim your dignity and restore peace. Do this for the same reason you would apologize to a friend if you had

Prescription for alleviating conflict

If your husband is short-tempered with the children, check to see if you've been respectful. The quickest way to restore harmony for the whole family is to make apologies where you have been disrespectful.

hurt her feelings. Once you apologize, there's a chance he'll soften. He might even follow your example and apologize to the children himself. From there, if you continue to reinforce that what daddy says goes, he'll have less to prove. Again, you are not responsible for how your husband treats the children, but you can certainly influence him.

"I praise loudly, I blame

softly."

— Catherine II of Russia

Birds Do It. Bees Do It. Why Don't We Ever Do It?

CHAPTER

8

Sex in a marriage is one of the most spiritual ways that we remind ourselves who we are. Something mystical and inexplicable happens when couples bring their energy together and merge physically. In my experience, when the wife is surrendering to her husband, this experience is even more intense and satisfying for both partners. There are a few obvious reasons for this.

For one thing, most men would rather not have sex with their mothers, and that's who we remind them of when we're controlling them and telling them what to do. By contrast, a respectful wife is far more attractive to her husband because he knows he will not be criticized or ridiculed. He knows his wife appreciates his masculinity. Such a man is more likely to be proactive with lovemaking, and the couple may have sex more frequently as a result.

When a wife relinquishes control of when, how, and where sex happens in the couplehood, she is free to focus on receiving. She can show up with her vulnerability. In response to this, the man may feel more inclined to be tender and generous with his wife. The more he gives her, the more likely she will feel grateful and satisfied. If she expresses this gratitude, the man feels appreciated and is likely to give even more. Thus, surrendering has a very positive effect in the bedroom.

On another level, this physical union is intensified because opposites attract. The greater the differences, the greater the attraction. If you make love to your husband with a very feminine spirit, the contrast to his masculinity provides greater drama and passion. Just as our bodies are perfectly and intricately designed to fit together and bring each other pleasure, a feminine and masculine spirit utterly complement each other.

"You Jane. Me Tarzan."

— Tarzan

Most couples start their relationship with plenty of gender contrast, which is part of the reason that sex is so exciting when you first start out the relationship. Another reason it's exciting initially is that, typically, both of you were sexually starved for some period of time before the relationship started. Add to it the novelty of a new sex partner, and you've got some pretty intense sex happening. At this point, nobody is saying they have a headache or they're too tired. Everybody is showing up eager for sex. Then the novelty wears off, and you realize that since you can have sex whenever you want it, you don't have to have it every single day. If, in addition, the gender contrast has diminished as you've become more controlling (a masculine characteristic) and he's started taking less initiative (a feminine characteristic), suddenly, even reruns of Gilligan's Island are more appealing than lovemaking.

It's hard to have your partner seem novel again when you've been together for years, and if you're having sex on a regular basis, your appetite is less voracious. Still, surrendering has a way of increasing the excitement in the bedroom because it adjusts your gender contrast to "high." Since you're the woman, come to the bedroom (or kitchen or laundry room) as female as possible. That means being soft, delicate and receptive. Wearing something feminine never hurts either.

In general, a surrendered wife says yes when her husband offers her sex regardless of whether she's in the mood or not. This is not to say that she's a doormat. There are certain circumstances, which I'll describe in a minute, where you should refuse your husband, but not being in the mood isn't one of them. Moods come and moods go, and as you know, just because you don't start out in the mood to have sex doesn't mean you won't end up there before it's over. There's nothing wrong with offering him your body or, at least, the chance to try to talk you into it when he wants to make love with you. This is a good rule of thumb for several reasons: For one thing, you get that physical connection we talked about earlier. For another thing, agreeing to make love with your husband helps make him feel loved. Not least of all, withholding sex as a bargaining chip in the relationship is very damaging to intimacy. Saying yes whenever you can is a good way to ensure that you avoid the chilling effect of a sexual power struggle.

"That's enough, and

enough is too much!"

— Popeye

How Much is Enough?

In theory, all you have to do to have a great sex life is be respectful and wear something sheer and lacy. That's a good start, but even with that, a mutually satisfying sex life in a marriage can be elusive. Rare is the marriage where both parties are completely satisfied with the frequency of sex. In Woody Allen's movie Annie Hall, he complains to his therapist that they hardly ever do it—only two, maybe three times a week. At the same time, she is complaining to her therapist that they do it all the time—two, maybe three times a week!

In my own marriage, I made the mistake of telling my husband that I didn't think we were making love enough and that I wanted him to initiate it more. As you can imagine, this did absolutely nothing to enhance our sex life or increase the frequency. Without batting an eye, John told me he would add "have sex with Laura" to his list of chores–right between "take out the trash" and "weed the garden." Clearly he felt I was making a demand for him to perform somehow, and he didn't like it.

Next, I decided that I would simply take matters into my own hands by suggesting that we have sex when the moment seemed right. This was also an unsuccessful tactic because it was simply another attempt to control the situation. In response, my husband seemed reluctant and disinterested. Finally, I decided I would focus strictly on receiving from him sexually instead of making demands.

Slowly things shifted in our relationship. After some time had passed, my husband noticed I was no longer making demands on him in this area. He started to initiate sex more, and as he did, I realized why I was so invested in controlling our sex life. I felt my own terror come up as I recognized I was definitely not in control of when or how we made love. As I focused on just receiving and responding according to my instincts instead of my need to control, I felt quite vulnerable. Ironically, this seemed attractive to my husband, who responded with even more masculine prowess. I did the best I could to keep breathing and remember that I was with a man who loved me and wanted me to be happy. I tried to remember that I was safe and tried to enjoy being pursued and desired.

Prescription for more frequent lovemaking

Make yourself sexually available to your husband at least once a week. This will not be as effective if mixed with disrespect and criticism. For best results, apologize as necessary first.

ARE YOU SAYING I SHOULDN'T ASK MY HUSBAND FOR SEX?

Asking my husband for sex was generally about trying to control him or at least trying to control the situation, which didn't work for me. The women in the Surrendered Circle had similar experiences. If you find it works for you, more power to you. If not, there are some other ways to get the ball rolling when you're in the mood.

Instead of demanding or requesting sex, make yourself available to receive sexually at a time when you're both available. There are hundreds of ways to do that, each with a varying degree of risk. Here are some examples:

1) Squeeze his arm and say "Oooh, you're strong."
2) Put on a negligee and lay on the bed with a book.
3) Tell him he looks sexy in those jeans and squeeze his butt.
4) Give him a long, slow kiss and a hug.
5) Snuggle up with him in bed.
6) Tell him that you're feeling especially erotic today.
7) Take off all your clothes and get into the bed or the shower with him.

Telling your husband you think the two of you should have more sex is much less scary, of course, because it's less vulnerable. The danger of making yourself available is that you *could* be rejected. Anything short of an enthusiastic response will be disappointing especially if your intentions are unmistakable. On the other hand, if he responds enthusiastically, you are now at risk of getting what you wanted in the first place—sexual intimacy with your husband. That can be scary too. Because of these inherent risks, it's tempting to just "forget" to make yourself available. I know it's hard to arrange your schedule and find time, but try to do it at least once a week just to stay in practice.

I really had a hard time with this concept because I struggled with the fear on both sides—fear of being rejected and fear of being approached. I couldn't figure out which was worse. Although I hate to admit it, I was very tempted to just avoid the whole thing by concocting a headache or saying I was sleepy. I wanted to avoid any situation that might result in a physical connection just so I wouldn't have to feel so terrified. But why should I be

"If you don't like something, change it. If you can't change it, change your attitude. Don't complain."

— Maya Angelou

afraid to make love to my own husband? This puzzled me for some time, but when I started discussing my ambivalence with other women, I soon learned I wasn't the only one. As I shared and listened to other wives talking honestly about their sex lives, I began to notice a common theme.

JUST SAY NO

"The art of love is largely the art of persistence."

— Albert Ellis

In Jeanine's case, her husband Carl seemed to always be after her. She felt continuously pressured and spent a lot of energy avoiding the whole issue. As she began surrendering and practiced receiving from her husband, she decided to make a commitment to make love with her husband at least once a week whether she felt like it or not. She likened it to doing the laundry or any other chore that she didn't particularly like. "I may not feel like doing it at the time, but afterwards, the clothes are clean," she told me. Without mentioning anything to Carl, Jeanine picked a night of the week as "laundry night."

Once Jeanine did this, she noticed that the pressure she felt from her husband was alleviated. He wasn't hanging on her as much, and she was less likely to view his casual hugs and kisses as a threat. It started out as a discipline, but this regular commitment helped her feel more bonded to her husband.

Still, there came a day when this plan was no longer working for Jeanine. Once her husband knew that Saturday nights were a pretty sure thing, she again started to feel pressured. Days before, she was already starting to dread it because, in her mind, she now had no choice in the matter.

Jeanine was not unique in her fear. Among the women in the Circle, most of us had an underlying belief that we had to have sex with our husbands if we went past a certain point. We had all exercised our right to say, "not tonight," but this was something more. We shared an overly simplistic, black-and-white view of sex that made us feel we were either going to do it and go all the way, or we weren't going to engage at all. Once we acquiesced to a kiss, or got undressed or passed some other symbolic starting point, there was no turning back.

The way this sense of obligation manifests is usually just as it did with Jeanine—Reluctance to engage in any physical contact at all. The reasoning goes something like this:

1) If I kiss him, he might get turned on.
2) If he gets turned on, he'll want to have sex with me.
3) If he wants to have sex with me, I'll have to because I got him aroused in the first place.
4) I may not want to have sex with him, so if I want to keep my options open...
5) I won't kiss him—at least not like *that!*

The problem with this thinking is that it also prevents us from engaging in sensual activities that don't necessarily culminate in an orgasm. Erotic pleasures like back rubs, showering together, or playing strip poker seem too threatening to enjoy. If you avoid these activities because you're afraid you'll owe something, practice receiving sexually from your husband. This may be difficult at first. Fortunately, there's a way to walk through this process of enjoying physical intimacy with your husband without controlling him.

YOUR SEXUAL BILL OF RIGHTS

To set the record straight once and for all, *you always have the option to tell your husband that you're not available for sex at that moment.* In fact, for a mutually fulfilling sex life, you must honor your own feelings and limitations by excusing yourself when necessary. You can do this at any point during a sexual encounter: while you're

"Welcome anything that comes to you, but do not long for anything else."

— *Andre Gide*

kissing, after you're undressed, and once you've started. Your husband may be disappointed or angry, but that is not your concern. When you feel unavailable, say, "I'm not available right now." Even if you've already kissed or hugged or started intercourse or other activities.

Having said that, I also suggest that you say yes whenever you can. That may sound like a contradiction, but it really isn't. A surrendered wife makes herself available as often as possible, but is quick to say no when she's not available. But what's the difference? How can you tell one from the other? Only you will know, so take a minute to check with yourself in the moment. For instance, if you're drifting off to sleep and your husband initiates lovemaking, you might feel some resistance to the idea of waking up. However, once you get started, you'll probably enjoy the encounter. Although you may not be thrilled with the idea at first, this would be a good time to connect with your husband physically.

On the other hand, if your husband initiates lovemaking and you immediately feel obligation or pressure to perform, I would suggest you let him know you're not available. If you're thinking that you always feel pressured to perform when your husband approaches you sexually, take a look at the underlying fear. What are your beliefs about the rules of sex? Here are some of the beliefs about sex that I've heard from wives:

- "If I don't have sex with him, he'll look for it someplace else."
- "If I don't have sex with him, he won't see how fat/ freckled/wrinkled/sweaty I am."
- "If I don't have sex with him now, he won't approach me again."
- "If I don't have sex with him when he wants to, he won't love me."

"The best proof of love is trust."

— Joyce Brothers

- "If I have sex with him and it's only so-so, he'll complain that it's not as good as it used to be."
- "If I don't have sex with him, he'll be angry at me and I will feel guilty."
- "If I have sex with him, I'll have to satisfy him even if I don't want to."

If you find yourself identifying with one or more of these beliefs, you are certainly not alone; however, they aren't enhancing the intimacy in your marriage. What I have learned by comparing notes with other women is that these fears motivate us to try to control or manipulate our situation. I'm not suggesting that your feelings of fear are not important, or that you should simply try to overcome them. I *am* saying that it's not in your best interest to act on your fear. Unfortunately, controlling and manipulating keeps us from connecting and leaves us feeling lonely.

So what should you do? Start by examining your fears and see if they are justifiable or not. If you believe that you must have sex with your husband once the ball gets rolling, I want you to sit down and write a letter to yourself. In this letter, I want you to explain to yourself that you don't ever have to have sex when you don't want to. It might look something like this:

Dear Self,
I'm sorry that I've been pressuring you to have sex when you didn't want to. I know that felt terrible, and I want you to know that I'll never do that to you again. From now on, if you don't want to do anything, you don't have to do anything. You can even change your mind after we've already started. I promise I'll always listen to you, no matter what.

Love,
Me

"The hardest of all is learning to be a well of affection, and not a fountain; to show them we love them not when we feel like it, but when they do."

— Nan Fairbrother

"The definition of a beau-

tiful woman is one who

loves me."

— *Sloan Wilson*

Now that you've made this promise to yourself, you need to keep it. To set the stage for honoring this agreement, let your husband know that you're working on some issues of your own that may make you unavailable for sex for the time being. Ask him to please bear with you. Let him know that you still think he's attractive and this has nothing to do with him. Tell him you'll let him know when you're available again. He might continue to approach you in the meantime, and in each moment you will get to decide whether you're available or not.

When Gina told her husband this, she was so nervous about it she couldn't make eye contact. She found herself looking at the ground, shaking with fear. Her husband was tender with her and responded by telling her that he loved her— no matter what— and wanted to protect her. Carrie had a similar experience with her husband, who when asked if he would bear with her for a while said, "Of course, I will."

If you're thinking that your husband would never respond that way, you are not alone. Gina and Carrie were both surprised. You will probably be pleasantly surprised too. The reason I say that is because telling your husband about this part of you is a very vulnerable thing to do. It demonstrates a degree of trust and faith in him that he will not want to disappoint. He is also likely to find the vulnerability attractive, and like Gina's husband, he may feel an urge to protect you.

If, when you tell this to your husband, he asks you how long it will be, tell him you're not sure but that you are definitely trying to work it out as quickly as possible. Ideally you will feel the desire to return to a sexual relationship with your husband. At the end of three months, if you're still feeling unavailable, you may need to go see a therapist to work through your fears. Remember that the primary difference between your relationship with your husband and your relationship with everybody else is that you are sexual with him. If that piece is missing, you should work very hard to reclaim it.

Let's take a look at some of the beliefs that keep us from being truly intimate with our husbands:

1. *If I don't have sex with him, he'll look for it someplace else.*

As long as your husband is not a sex addict who is acting out with other women, you have nothing to worry about. (If he is a sex addict acting out with other women, see the section in chapter one called "When to stop surrendering.")

Your husband may very well need more sex than you are able to offer him, particularly if you're unavailable for a while. Fortunately, men know exactly how to satisfy themselves when no one else is available, so trust that he will know how to take care of himself by himself. He probably went longer than three months without sex plenty of times before he met you. A temporary break in sexual relations with you is not going to drive him into some other woman's bed. Remind yourself of this when you feel afraid.

If your husband has a history of infidelity this may be harder to come to terms with, but, if he has the capacity to be faithful, he can certainly go without sex for three months or longer. What he can't go without for long is respect and admiration. Ongoing control and criticism are far more dangerous threats to monogamy than the absence of sex.

Some women feel threatened when their husbands masturbate, but men tend to view masturbating as a bodily function, like urinating, rather than a cataclysmic sexual ex-

"We all suffer from the preoccupation that there exists...in the loved one, perfection."

— Sidney Portier

perience. There's an old joke which says that studies show that 98% of all men masturbate and the other 2% lie. Your husband is probably like most men. He may even use pornography when he masturbates. If you ever saw this pornography, you would probably find it tasteless and offensive, or perhaps you would feel inadequate and jealous. Either way, what he's reading or watching is strictly between him and God, and it's none of your business. A centerfold is not the same as a flesh-and-bones woman, so don't make it more than it is. Remember that part of the reason he's attracted to you is because he's attracted to the female form. That's the way he's made.

"You must be the change you wish to see in the world."

— Mahatma Gandhi

You may find these views on the topics of masturbation and pornography outrageous or overly permissive, but keep in mind that you can't control your husband's masturbating or pornography viewing. Trying to stop him is not only a waste of time, it interferes with your intimacy. So even if you completely disagree with my perspective, try to remember the bigger picture: Control and intimacy are mutually exclusive. If you want the latter, you must give up the former, including and especially in the area of sex.

2. *"If I have sex with him, I'll have to work hard to prevent him from seeing how fat/freckled/wrinkled/sweaty I am."*

You haven't showered all day, yet your husband is making goo-goo eyes that tell you he's ready to do the wild thing. You can hardly believe he would find someone with greasy hair attractive, so you refuse him, right? Instead, I suggest you jump at the opportunity to connect.

If your husband finds you attractive enough to have sex with, it is not in your best interest to refuse him because you don't *feel* attractive. For one thing, you're acting on the belief that this man has bad taste, when clearly he has excellent taste as evidenced by the fact that he married you. For another thing, you're criticizing what he thinks is attractive, which is not a very surrendered thing to do.

Passing up an opportunity to have a physically intimate moment with your husband because you feel inadequate is no good for anybody. You're denying yourself the chance to receive pleasure and feel beautiful in his arms. You're denying him the chance to give you pleasure. You're passing up the connection, the magic and the sensuality. All because you feel insecure about your body.

Instead, I suggest that you pretend that you feel beautiful, even if you don't, and graciously receive his offer. Try not to flinch if he fondles your stomach, or looks at your thighs, or runs his fingers through your dirty hair. Don't stand between your husband and what he finds pleasurable. Don't worry about how you smell or what bodily fluids you've excreted. If he doesn't care, why should you? I know that what I'm suggesting is difficult, but if you practice this, you will remove a barrier to intimacy with your husband. You will even start to feel attractive at times that you never thought you would.

3. *"If I don't have sex with him now, he won't approach me again."*

While it's true that repeated rejections can be discouraging, it's not likely to make your husband stop trying. For one thing, random reinforcement is very powerful. As an analogy, a slot machine in Las Vegas pays off sometimes but not others, but plenty of people keep trying. If you have told your husband up front that you might not be available and that it's not about him, he probably won't take your rejection personally. Another reason he won't stop trying is that part of his physical makeup drives him to mate with

"A man is already halfway in love with any woman who listens to him."

— Brendan Francis

"Perfect love is rare

indeed—for to be a lover

will require that you

continually have the

subtlety of the very wise,

the flexibility of the child,

the sensitivity of the artist,

the understanding of the

philosopher, the

acceptance of the saint, the

tolerance of the scholar

and the fortitude of the

certain."

— Leo Buscaglia

you. His instincts tell him to plant his seed.

If your husband is not approaching you, a much more significant problem may be rejection outside the bedroom. He may be reacting to feeling disrespected, dismissed, controlled, or criticized. Keep working on respecting him and deferring to his thinking, and practice making yourself available to him.

4. *"If I don't have sex with him when he wants to, he won't love me."*

This belief reflects a painful lack of self-worth. If you feel this way, you are seriously discounting your own gifts and talents. You forget that your husband loves you for lots of reasons—like the way you mother his children, make a home, throw a party, admire his muscles, or cry at movies. Remind yourself that you have intrinsic value as a person, not just as a sex partner. Your husband did not marry you just for the sex. For that, he could have gotten something that required much less maintenance.

A reasonable man will not insist on having sex when you're not available. He may complain loudly, but he won't stop loving you because you're taking a temporary break from having sex with him. Keep in mind that he wants you to be happy, and if that means entertaining himself for a while, so be it.

It is completely reasonable for him to want you to have sex when he wants it, but his love for you doesn't depend on it. You are lovable whether you are performing sexually or not.

5. *"If I have sex with him and it's only so-so, he'll complain that it's not as good as it used to be."*

Anticipating your husband's reaction is counter to being intimate with him. Every second you spend thinking about what he's probably going to do or say is another second that you miss interacting and connecting with him. Seconds turn into minutes, which turn into hours and days. Avoid dwelling on thoughts that start with the word "if." They take you out of the moment and away from your husband. Some women miss their entire marriage this way.

"You don't love a woman because she is beautiful, but she is beautiful because you love her."

— Anonymous

Even if you could anticipate his reaction, how do you know the sex is only going to be so-so? You might end up having terrific sex when you least expect it. Remember the point of lovemaking is to connect physically, remind yourself who you are and to distinguish your marriage relationship from every other relationship you have in the world. Not all sex is fabulous, so don't hold yourself to an impossible standard.

6. "If I don't have sex with him, he'll be angry at me and I will feel guilty."

If you have been rejecting your husband for some time, you are neglecting your responsibility to be sexual in the marriage. Find a good counselor and get to work on this problem as soon as possible. Apologize to your husband for depriving him sexually, and tell him you are doing everything you can to get to the root of the problem and heal it so you'll be available for him.

On the other hand, if you find yourself unavailable only occasionally, you have every right to refuse him and offer a rain check. He may be angry or disappointed or frustrated with you, but that is not your responsibility. You are better off honoring your own spirit than trying to meet his needs when you really don't feel comfortable. The price of not honoring yourself in this situation is generally resentment, anxiety, crankiness, and vindictiveness. Those feelings will strain the intimacy in your marriage, making everybody lonely.

7. *"If I start to have sex with him, I'll have to satisfy him even if I don't want to."*

Prescription for improved sexual response

To demonstrate to yourself that you are in charge of your own body when it comes to lovemaking, ask your husband to stop after sex has begun. He may object, try to talk you out of it or stall, but a good guy won't force you. If you want, you can resume after he stops.

Women with sexual abuse in their past especially tend to feel this way, and understandably so. If you've survived a rape, date rape, statutory rape or molestation, you probably identify with this belief. What these experiences hold in common is that saying "no" is not an option. You learn that you have no choice.

If your husband is one of the good guys as described in the first chapter, then he is not one of the creeps that forced you. Remind yourself that he never will be. When you ask a good guy (i.e., your husband) to stop in the middle of lovemaking, he may protest, but he won't rape you. The truth is, you always have a choice, and knowing that will make you feel freer to engage in lovemaking.

TAKING CARE OF YOURSELF FIRST

But what if your husband is not approaching you as much as you might like? Patty's story illustrates the importance of staying focused on our own self-care in this situation instead of trying to manipulate or make demands.

One evening when Patty's husband came home from work, she found herself wishing he would approach her for lovemaking. Instead of saying anything, she asked herself what it was she needed. The answer was a nap. She announced that she was going to lie down for a while. When she woke up two hours later, her husband had put the kids to bed and washed the dishes. Patty felt refreshed and grateful. When her husband came to bed shortly thereafter, he wanted to have sex with her, so she agreed.

Had Patty not taken the nap, she would have felt tired and less available. Had she asked for sex, her husband might have felt controlled and resentful. The moral of the story is, as with all surrendering, to put your own needs first and let go of the results.

"You will find as you look back upon your life that the moments when you have truly lived are the moments when you have done things in the spirit of love."

— Henry Drummond

Resisting The Really Big Bait

Becoming a surrendered wife is difficult because it requires that we break well-worn, lifelong habits. Even worse, your husband may also fight you every step of the way since you will be disrupting some of his lifelong habits as well. If he is used to you being his mom, he will protest loudly when you start relinquishing control of things and leaving them in his lap. He will do this even if he doesn't consciously know you are doing anything differently. His chief weapon will be Really Big Bait.

Really Big Bait is anything that will get you to respond in the old way. It makes you want to engage in a familiar conversation or argument. For instance, let's say you've given up control of the finances and you're letting him take care of the bills. The very next thing you know, your husband may come bursting into the room with an important announcement such as "I don't know how we're going to pay the mortgage this month!"

Make no mistake about it: This announcement is an engraved invitation for you to jump up and do the same old dance that you've been doing together for years. He is trying to get you to engage. You might be tempted to say, "Let me take a look at the numbers," or "How much are we short by?" or "Take some money out of the savings then." If you offer any of those answers, or a number of others that quickly come to mind, you are in effect saying, "I wasn't really serious about giving up the checkbook. Forget the whole thing and I'll take it over again. That way I won't have to be terrified, and you won't have to be uncomfortable."

"Few things can help an individual more than to place responsibility on him, and to let him know that you trust him."

— Booker T. Washington

Really Big Bait can come in a number of forms. He might ask your opinion about whether he should go back to school, get a nose job, or how he should handle a situation at work. The truth is, in each of those situations, he needs to do what he thinks is best, even if you're afraid you'll never see him during the semester or that he can't afford plastic surgery or that he'll lose his job. As long as you're worried about those things for him, he knows he doesn't have to worry and that you don't believe in him. When you let go of his worries (or at least act like you're letting go), he has to pick them up again himself. With no mom to dump his troubles on and take directions from, he's going to have to figure things out for himself. This is a good thing, as he'll have more success running his own life than you would have running it for him.

Your husband might also try to engage you without saying a word. He might let bills stack up in a box without even opening them and ignore calls on the answering machine from creditors. He might quit his job and make no movement towards getting another one for some time. He might let the baby cry for much longer than you are comfortable with. You can engage with him by jumping in and saving the day. Suddenly, he no longer has to worry about creditors or jobs or babies because, thankfully, you're taking care of all of that for him. Once again you are the mom, and he sees that you don't really believe he'll take care of things.

So what do you do when your husband brings out

Really Big Bait? It's a perfect opportunity to trust. If he's using verbal bait, affirm that you believe in him, that you know he'll figure it out, and that you aren't worried about it because you know he's handling it. But what if you don't believe in him at all and you're almost positive he's screwing up? Tell him you believe in him and trust him as an affirmation to yourself, to help you become the vulnerable, intimate wife that you want to be. Tell him as a way of mirroring back to him his own capabilities and confidence, however difficult they are to see. Say it with all the conviction you can muster because it is a magic formula that will change you both for the better.

    If your husband tries to get you to dance the old dance or uses silent bait, call a friend and vent your fears, but smile when you see him and thank him for all he's doing. It's especially important that you not mention the bait. Once you say, "I see you've got quite a stack of bills there," you've just engaged. Now he can breathe a sigh of relief knowing that you are worrying about the bills so he doesn't have to.

    Another form of Really Big Bait is the verbal punch. Your husband may attempt to get you to spar with him by throwing the first punch so you'll hit him back. Then the two of you will be in the unpleasant but familiar territory of a brawl. It's instinctive to want to hit back to protect yourself but I don't recommend it. If you do, the very best case scenario is that you'll end up hurting him back, and you will both be hurt and defensive when you stop. Worst case scenario is a full-blown war where you both walk away wounded.

    So instead of responding in kind, tell him how you feel by saying "ouch!" when he verbally punches you. That's it. Just say ouch, then walk away. You don't need to explain why that hurt your feelings or demand an apology

"Courage is not the absence of fear, but rather the judgment that something else is more important than fear."

— Ambrose Redmoon

or say anything else.

When I suggest this, some women complain that it sounds goofy to them. What they're really saying is it feels too vulnerable. Saying "ouch" is as good as telling your husband he made a direct hit to your jugular. Part of us wants to conceal this information because we don't want him to know where our jugular is—it's too dangerous. The truth is, your husband already knows where your weaknesses are. Saying "ouch" is not giving him any new information. While he may seem like the enemy in the heat of battle, he's not. You're both on the same team. Showing him a soft underbelly is a good way to remind him of this.

Sometimes it's so shocking to get punched, you won't remember to say ouch. You'll just realize you're incredibly mad at your husband. Underneath that anger is the sadness and the hurt. You may not be in touch with it while you're still smarting, but it's there. If you stick with the hurt instead of lashing out in anger, you are taking an important step towards being vulnerable. Vulnerability is far more courageous than defensiveness and anger, and you must be vulnerable to be intimate.

Once again, your husband will hear only his own voice of conviction when you don't scream at him or complain about what he's done. He'll also feel sheepish about trying to start a fight when you don't play the game with him. Chances are, he'll be more cautious about doing it again if he doesn't get the reaction he was looking for.

Armed with this information, Brenda decided to give this approach a try. She was in the heat of a battle with her husband when she suddenly stopped and responded to what he said with a loud "ouch!" When she told me about this later, she said she was disappointed that she had not gotten an apology from her husband. It was new for Brenda to express this vulnerability, and she was so terrified that

"I cannot say whether things will get better if we change; what I can say is they must change if they are to get better."

— *G.C. Lichtenberg*

she was ready to give up the whole idea after only one try when it didn't "work."

I reminded Brenda that the goal of expressing her hurt was to avoid engaging in emotional bloodshed with her husband and to stay intimate–not necessarily to elicit an apology from him. Since Brenda had already thrown some slime at her husband prior to saying "ouch," he was probably too busy protecting himself to worry about her feelings. Instead of giving up when she didn't get an apology, I encouraged her to work on bringing her vulnerability to her husband *before* the counterattack.

In the meantime, Brenda was wise to find another outlet for her hurt feelings. Calling a girlfriend to talk about how your husband hurt you is a good idea. Find someone who is a good listener and supports you in surrendering. If you can't process with a friend, do some writing in a journal about your pain. Otherwise, chances of that hurt finding it's way out of your mouth in the form of a nasty comment are high.

Saying ouch when your husband hurts your feelings is a good habit to get into for the sake of intimacy and emotional honesty in your marriage. When you succeed, congratulate yourself on not engaging in a destructive pattern. As a fringe benefit, you may eventually get an apology. In the meantime, you will have kept your dignity by not resorting to throwing insults and raised the standards in the relationship by not taking the Really Big Bait.

HOW DO YOU SPELL "BAIT?"

Of course, not all bait is really big. Some bait is small, but just as tempting. For instance, if your husband asks you for a phone number you don't know off the top of your head, resist the temptation to look it up in the phone book for him. Resist the temptation to tell him there's such

"You are always on your way to a miracle."

— *Sark*

a thing as a phone book. Don't hesitate to say, "I don't know" when you don't. That same phrase, or even silence, is a good response for bait like this:

When is the car registration due?

Which frying pan should I use?

What should I order for breakfast?

Where should I park?

How much should I leave for a tip?

Telling your husband that you'll go along with whatever he thinks is a powerful way to deflect bait and remind him that you're not interested in doing any of the old dances. You are also forcing him to meet new challenges, which will have positive side-effects. He's going to have to come up with his own solutions and feel his own sense of accomplishment and pride when he meets those challenges. The less you provide solutions, the more he has to think for himself. The more he accomplishes, the better he feels about himself, and the more he feels capable of taking on the new tasks. The benefit for you is that the more you relinquish inappropriate control of things, the less stress you have, and the more intimacy.

The only time you wouldn't want to refer your husband back to his own thinking is if he's asking you to choose something based on your desires, such as where you want to go to dinner, what color car you like, or which apartment you'd rather live in. Go ahead and say what you prefer. If, however, he asks you which computer he should buy, how to dress the baby, or whether or not to refinance the mortgage, use the phrase "Whatever you think."

You may find yourself exasperated when your husband invites you to advise him over and over again. You may resist the bait the first eight times, only to give in the ninth time he asks the same question. Fortunately, as with practicing any of the principles of a surrendered wife, you

Prescription for peace of mind

If your husband asks you what to do, always deflect the question by encouraging him to do whatever he thinks he should do. Do your best to avoid giving him advice, even if he asks for it.

don't have to be perfect. Soon your husband will learn not to ask you about things that he can figure out for himself. Continue to exercise your 'surrendering' muscles, and you too will learn not to engage.

If you and your husband are accustomed to doing a dance where you punish him for making certain mistakes, then things are going to feel very weird when you stop doing that. With the old system, once you had a hissy-fit, he could justify his behavior in his own mind by reasoning that you're no picnic to live with. He could also focus on defending himself from your wrath instead of feeling the consequences of his actions. In the meantime, you would have lost your dignity and grace by giving in to the temptation to dress him down.

One example of this is what happened with Joan and Kevin. When Kevin knew he had done something to anger Joan, he would skulk around the house, waiting for her to yell at him so they could have a blow-out and be done with it. When Joan decided it was no longer in her best interest to yell at him when he made a mistake, Kevin squirmed, paced, and baited her. When she still didn't yell at him and he didn't have to defend himself against her, he suddenly heard his own voice loud and clear. The weight of his guilt was much more uncomfortable than a fight with his wife.

Your husband may also "like" to be punished so he doesn't have to feel his own guilt. Instead, I urge you to remain dignified and serene. In most cases, you can express your feelings in one short sentence, like "I'm angry that you didn't come home when you said you would." That's a far cry from "You're always late and you never do what you say you're going to do! I wish you would think about someone besides yourself once in a while! I don't know why I believe you when you say you're going to do something!"

"To fall in love is easy, even to remain in it is not difficult; our human loneliness is cause enough. But it is a hard quest worth making to find a comrade through whose steady presence one becomes steadily the person one desires to be."

— Anna Louise Strong

Now that you recognize bait and know when he's inviting you to engage, you may get irritated when you spot it. You might think, "If he would just stop baiting me, I would stop controlling him!" However, it doesn't seem to work that way. If you want things to change, you're going to have to change first.

THE ENERGY SURPLUS

Prior to surrendering, most of the wives had spent a lot of time and energy in Needless Emotional Turmoil, or NET for short. Once we stopped worrying about our husbands, we suddenly had an energy surplus that felt unfamiliar and even uncomfortable. Some of us experienced a sense of loss. For instance, shortly after she began surrendering, Susan was not sure what to do with all her freetime. Carolyn realized that since she wasn't going to talk about money, she had nothing to talk about when she went out to dinner with her husband.

If surrendering makes you feel like you can't say anything and you have nothing to do, that's a good measure of how much time you spent in Needless Emotional Turmoil. Without NET, life can be downright boring. There's no more obsessing about money. There's no more telling him what to do. There's no more telling him about things you think he should have done differently. There isn't as much drama or fighting. It can be dull, dull, dull.

As an analogy, think of a backpack that holds all of your concerns for your husband. Imagine you are putting on this backpack every day and suddenly you stop. You will feel a little weightless at first. Maybe you would go to the spot where you used to put the backpack on every day and just look at it out of habit. Then as you make the choice to leave it where it is rather than putting it on, you might feel awkward and strange, as well as light and unburdened. Throughout the day little surges of panic would pulse

"You yourself, as much as anybody in the entire universe, deserve your love and affection."

— *Buddha*

through your body when you notice you're not wearing the backpack, as if it contained something valuable and you left it on the bus. Remind yourself that you're not supposed to be wearing that backpack, and that it's okay to leave it off. Notice how much more you can do without it, how much faster you can move when you're not wearing it.

When you first experience an energy surplus from not wearing a worry-filled backpack, you may also notice another feeling coming up. For example, you may feel you have nothing in common with your husband anymore. Perhaps you'll have some dissatisfaction with some other aspect of your life, like your children or home or career. When that happens, be sure to pat yourself on the back for doing such a good job surrendering. If you're feeling tongue-tied and restless, it's probably because you're doing a good job resisting the temptation to wear the backpack. This is a good thing! You're making progress.

As soon as you finish patting yourself on the back, start a new project immediately. Make a quilt or a new friend. Read a novel, or write one of your own. Join a gym or a club. Take a class or take a trip. Do something that interests you, even if it means getting a baby-sitter or spending money. Do this especially if you think you don't have time. Pick a project that really interests you and delights your spirit. Put that extra energy into something you enjoy.

What does doing something you enjoy have to do with being intimate with your husband? For one thing, getting involved in your own life distracts you so you won't be as tempted to take a bite of Really Big Bait. More importantly, your new project will make you happy and awaken your passion. When you're happy, you're more fun to be around. You're more likely to be grateful and respectful instead of nit-picky and critical. You'll also feel more alive and excited, accomplished and creative. Plus, you'll have something to talk about at dinner.

"Fear is that little darkroom where negatives are developed."

— Michael Pritchard

Prescription for greater happiness

Make a list of ten projects, hobbies or activities that you enjoy. Circle one, then make a call, a purchase or a plan to get started on it right away.

This may seem like a trivial point, but it's not. Unless you start to fill your time with things that feed your spirit, you will have a terrible time surrendering to your husband. Therefore, a key ingredient to a healthy, intimate marriage is having your own passions, even if your husband does not share them. If you love skiing and he doesn't, join a ski club and go every chance you get. If you enjoy foreign films and he hates subtitles, go with a friend. If you need to rumba and he hates to dance, sign up for a dance class at the local college.

As a wonderful fringe benefit to making yourself happy, you will also be making someone else you love happy: your husband. He will never feel better about himself or more attracted to you than when he sees you smiling, fulfilled, and excited. He may even follow your example and pursue his own passions. Then he'll have something interesting to talk about at dinner too.

THE RED HERRING

In a mystery novel, the red herring is the misleading information that keeps the detective from discovering the truth. I have learned that when I'm worrying about something my husband is doing, I'm usually following a red herring. This effort to control someone else is actually a way to distract myself from what's happening in my life. For example, maybe I'm nervous about a deadline that's coming up, or I'm irritated with a client for not getting back to me right away. Perhaps I'm mad at a friend who said something that hurt my feelings. Whatever it is, I can pretty much eliminate my husband's driving from the list of usual suspects. Once I've done that, I can get to work on finding the real culprit—whatever is going on with *me*.

When Sharon called me to tell me that her husband was not spending enough time with their daughter, I sensed she was distracted by a red herring. She was sure that she had a legitimate gripe and was irritated with me for asking her what else was going on. Finally, she admitted that she was feeling upset about a fight she'd had with her sister. As we discussed it more, Sharon admitted that she was sad and scared about talking to her sister, even though she saw her frequently. This was a difficult topic for Sharon—one that she wanted to avoid. Focusing on her husband's shortcomings was a handy distraction.

"One's mind, once stretched by a new idea, never regains its original dimensions."

— Oliver Wendell Holmes

The cost of distracting herself this way was high, however. If she said something to her husband to try to change his behavior, she would alienate him. This would leave her feeling lonely—not to mention how awful she'd feel about herself for trying to control him. Not only that, she would also be no closer to solving her original problem—the conflict with her sister. Instead, we talked about how she could handle the situation with her sister and keep her griping to herself.

The next time I spoke to Sharon, she said she had a different perspective on the whole situation. She had reconciled with her sister and realized that her husband was actually quite attentive to their daughter. The huge concern she'd had the other day seemed like an overreaction now. Her husband had been very supportive in listening to her process the conflict with her sister. She no longer wanted to criticize him or "let him have it" about his parenting.

THE REAL MCCOY

Sometimes you'll have a complaint about your husband that is very legitimate. Perhaps he is chronically late, sloppy, cranky, insulting, or smelly. Sometimes you will want to berate him for one of his truly annoying habits. But how can you tell the difference between a red herring and a situation where you need to speak up?

If you find yourself with a new complaint that isn't something that usually bothers you, chances are it's a red herring. If you find yourself thinking about something small (he doesn't rinse out his coffee cups and they're gross), it's most likely a red herring. His habit may truly bug you, but it's not a big deal. Don't sweat the small stuff. There must be something more exciting happening in your life than that. Ask yourself what it is.

If, on the other hand, you find yourself with a complaint that you've had time and time again, and it's not that his socks never make it into the hamper, then you may have something to talk about. Once you eliminate other suspects and you're sure that you have an authentic problem with your husband, you should talk about it with another wife. Preferably, you would talk to a wife who is supportive of your marriage and surrendering to your husband.

Call a girlfriend and tell her how sad you feel that your husband hasn't approached you for sex in weeks, or that he hurt your feelings again, or that you're tired of being broke all the time. Your feelings of fear, sadness, hurt, and anger are real. Do not dismiss them. Do not try to pretend that they're not there. Express these feelings to yourself, your friends, or your therapist, or write them down because they are your feelings. Before you decided to surrender to your husband, you used to express those feelings to him indiscriminately. While that wasn't ideal for your marriage, expressing those emotions was good for your mental health. What I'm suggesting is that you continue to express the feelings and validate them outside of your marriage so that you can continue to act with faith in your husband.

In other words, don't squash your feelings. It won't work. I've tried it and it can't be done. Feelings demand an outlet. You can't wish them away or dismiss them. You have them for a reason, and the more you pay attention to them, the more you know about what fits for you and how to take care of yourself physically, emotionally, and spiritu-

Prescription for spiritual growth

Let your urge to control be a clue that you need to examine your feelings. When you find yourself thinking, "he's loading the dishwasher the wrong way," ask yourself how you are really feeling right at that moment. Call a friend who will listen to you and keep talking until you figure it out.

ally.

Obviously, there will be times when you need to address your husband directly to let him know that you are angry with him. Since most controlling wives tend to err on the side of saying too much, it's best to reason things out with someone else first. This is a good safeguard against raging inappropriately or making veiled attempts to control. If your complaint is legitimate, it can wait until you've discussed it with someone else. This is an important part of learning to communicate cleanly. I struggle with this myself because when I'm hot with anger, I don't want to wait for anything. I just want to let him have it!

Janet was careful to get some other input on her situation before she let her husband know that she was angry that he repeatedly made her late to choir practice by coming home late to take care of their son. She delivered a direct message by saying "When you come home late on Tuesday nights, I feel angry that I have to be late to choir practice." Then she left without further discussion.

When she came home later that night, still feeling good from all that singing and harmonizing, her husband was brooding. He baited her a few times, looking for the comfort of a familiar brawl. Janet was feeling too good to engage and simply rebuffed his comments that he was "such a loser" and "couldn't do anything right." Instead, she told him she appreciated him for providing her with the opportunity to participate in the choir. This took her husband off-guard, and they went to bed without an argument. The following week, he was home in plenty of time for Janet to make it to the start of choir practice. She thanked her husband for being so considerate of her.

If Janet had said, "You're always late and I'm sick of it!" or "Why don't you try being on time for a change!" her husband probably wouldn't have heard her request, much less taken it seriously. If she had taken the bait and

"Any change, even a change for the better, is always accompanied by drawbacks and discomforts."

— Arnold Bennett

engaged in an argument with him when she got home, the issue would not have rested so heavily on his mind. As it was, he probably heard his own guilty thoughts since there were no distractions to help him tune them out. Janet had a legitimate issue, and she handled it beautifully in terms of getting what she wanted and maintaining intimacy in her marriage. You can do this to, but you'll want to solicit the advice of another wife or two first.

GOING INTO BATTLE

You'll also want to resist bait that shows up outside of your home. If the landlord, the principal, the store clerk, or the city council is causing you grief, do your best not to engage. Instead, let your husband know that you're scared or need help and let him handle it. Instead of putting on a suit of armor, rely on him to go to battle when it's appropriate, then stand behind him for protection.

When Stephanie had an issue with the way the school was treating their son, she was so angry she marched down to the school herself to deal with it. This was a difficult situation, and she felt overwhelmed by it almost immediately. Finally, she remembered that her husband Joe was ready and willing to defend their son and that all she had to do was ask for help. Stephanie and Joe attended the next conference together, with Joe doing most of the talking. She noticed that his physical stature and crossed arms seemed to command a great deal of respect. Stephanie felt relief, and Joe felt proud of how he had protected both his wife and child.

Your husband would probably also feel proud to protect you, if you'll let him.

Prescription for preventing unnecessary arguments

If you're going to tell your husband you are angry or unhappy about something, talk to someone else about it first to get some clarity about it. Practice delivering your message so that you stick to the topic and don't throw punches.

Surrendered Wives Don't Read Minds

CHAPTER

10

One day, my friend Theresa called and told me that she knew her husband was mad at her. I asked her how she knew, and she told me that he had scowled at her. "Did he say why he was mad at you?" I asked.

"He didn't have to," she told me. "I know it's because he thinks I'm spending too much on therapy."

"How do you know?" I probed further.

"I just know how he is," she countered.

I identified with Theresa's perception that she could read her husband's mind. I had often presumed to "know" what my husband was thinking based on his grunting, slamming, disinterest, or other non-verbal signals. However, as a surrendered wife, I learned that much of my interpretation had been based on fear and assumption. When my husband scowled at me without saying anything, I assumed he was angry, just as Theresa did. When he failed to change a burnt-out light bulb for weeks, I assumed he was inconsiderate and oblivious. When he watched television shows I didn't care for, I assumed he had poor taste.

Unfortunately, my psychic abilities were not as accurate as I had thought. I was frequently wrong when I tried to interpret him. When I took the time listen to his reaction, I was often pleasantly surprised. Instead of regarding an

"If we don't change, we don't grow. If we don't grow, we aren't really living."

— *Gail Sheehy*

ambiguous face as a call to battle, I made a decision to do nothing until I was spoken to directly. If my husband had a bone to pick with me, I reasoned that he would tell me in a straightforward way.

When I made a conscious effort to stop drawing my own conclusions, I learned that the scowl I thought was for me was actually intended for my sister-in-law. The unchanged light bulb was his defiant response to my controlling comments. The tasteless television shows were popular not just with my husband, but with many other men I know and respect who seem to find entertainment in places I never could.

Unless your husband tells you something directly, don't assume it. Even if you're a bonafide clairvoyant, reading your husband's mind does little to enhance your relationship. As much as we might like to *think* we know what they're thinking and how they're feeling, this is a counterproductive practice. To the best of her ability, a surrendered wife is careful not to make problems where none exist. If your husband says he's mad at you, then it's safe to assume that he's mad. Otherwise, don't get ahead of yourself.

For instance, when my husband said that he liked his new job, I didn't believe him. I was noticing that he seemed drained and listless every night when he came home. I reasoned that this meant he was not being truthful. Later a friend asked me how he liked his job and I said, "He says he likes it." I might just as well have said, "He doesn't like it, but he says he does," which is not exactly respectful. Today, I try to remember that if he tells me something, my job is to believe him. Just as I "fake it till I make it" sometimes, he may be doing the same. I certainly don't want to contradict him.

WHAT'S WRONG WITH ASKING "WHAT'S WRONG?"

If your husband is unusually quiet or slams the door or offers some other non-verbal clue that he's upset, you may be tempted to ask him what's wrong. Don't do it! Unless he articulates with words that he is angry with you for some reason, assume that everything is fine. Let him grumble or stomp or do whatever he does without commenting. Keep in mind that the man is an adult with the ability to communicate what he needs or wants without any help from you. He may need to retreat for a while to figure things out. Let him. You need to stay focused on what *you* need and want, and articulate that. Any distraction from that focus—like wondering what's wrong with him—is not in your best interest.

"Do not dwell in the past, do not dream of the future, concentrate the mind on the present moment."

— Buddha

The other problem with inviting him to tell you what's wrong when he's acting up is that you're rewarding and welcoming his unpleasant behavior. When you indulge him that way, you put yourself right into the role of the mother of a temperamental child. Your husband then gets the starring role of the bratty kid.

This is a difficult dance to stay out of, particularly if it was previously part of the culture of your relationship. As tempting as it is, I assure you that nothing good will come from inviting him to tell you how he's feeling. Therefore, you may need to go to great lengths to avoid the whole situation. I recommend getting out of the house, making a call to a girlfriend, watching television, reading a book, or finding any other distraction you can think of. His mood will pass eventually. Your job is to wait it out without inviting him to talk about it.

ANTICIPATION IS MAKING YOU BORED

Along with interpreting our husbands, I have noticed that many of us pride ourselves with knowing how our husbands will react to a given situation. This can be dangerous because it eliminates the need to actually consult him. The logic goes something like this:

- I already know what he's going to say before I ask him, so I really don't need to ask him.
- I don't like the answer that I think he would have given if I had asked him.
- I am disappointed and angry with my husband because he didn't say the right thing when I *didn't* ask for his input.

Prescription for better conversations

Write down what you anticipate your husband will say if you tell him you want to go out to the movies. Then, tell him you want to go to the movies and write down what he actually says.

On the other hand, maybe you don't mind the answer you assume your husband will give, but you're completely *bored* with the fact that you always know what he's going to say and therefore never have to ask him. That one goes like this:

- I already know what he's going to say before I ask him, so I really don't have to ask him.
- This "same old, same old" thing sure is getting dull. I wish my husband would say something different once in a while.
- I am now bored with my husband because he would have said the same thing he always says *if* I had asked him.

In either example above, you are now irritated with your husband even though he has not even spoken to you! Anticipating your husband's reaction is a barrier to intimacy. Instead of seeing him, we see our own expectations or fears, which leaves us feeling lonely. A surrendered wife knows that she can't correctly anticipate her husband's every reaction, and therefore she needs to ask him what he thinks.

Another reason to avoid anticipating is that it will take you longer to see the shift in your husband's behavior as you begin to shift your behavior. If he is feeling disrespected or defensive, his behavior will change dramatically when he begins to feel respected and secure. If you are anticipating hostility or stinginess based on his reactions before you surrendered, you're likely to be entirely off-base. To stay in relationship with your husband, listen to his reactions instead of preparing an argument for what you imagine he is going to say. Focus on listening to his words instead of interpreting his tone and expression.

In my early marriage, I also had a habit of "interpreting" my husband for other people. He would say something, and I would pipe up and tell them what he meant. I actually thought I was being helpful, but what I was doing was demeaning him. When we went for marriage counseling, I even tried to tell the therapist what he was saying! Obviously, I don't recommend this. Now, I just get out the duct tape—double-strength, if necessary.

I also recommend that you stop buying clothes for your husband. It's fine to pick out a jacket or a shirt as a gift for his birthday or some other special occasion, but selecting and purchasing his wardrobe on a regular basis is yet another form of anticipating and controlling. You may know what he likes, or what looks good on him, but for the sake of intimacy, it's much better to let him shop for himself. If this is difficult for you, remember that you want to play the role of his wife, not his mother. It's also more exciting to be married to a flesh-and-blood man than it is to have your own life-size dress-up doll.

"I argue very well. Ask any of my remaining friends. I can win an argument on any topic, against any opponent. People know this, and steer clear of me at parties. Often, as a sign of their great respect, they don't even invite me."

— Dave Barry

The Sky is Darkest Just Before the Dawn

YOU CALL THIS PROGRESS?

Kim was having a terrible time in her first month of surrendering. She felt she was doing a poor job and that things were getting worse, not better. One day she asked her husband, Rick, how his day had been and he confessed that he'd gone to a gun shop in the next town. She was shocked that he would do something like that without telling her first, especially since he knew she objected to guns. Rick admitted that he had not told her where he was going beforehand because he did not want to invoke her wrath and anti-gun lecture. She called me to tell me how deceitful he had been.

When I asked Kim how she would have felt if her husband had gone somewhere to look at a new car without telling her, she realized that she wouldn't have cared much. The reason she was so upset with his so-called deceit was because she realized her husband was not letting her control him like he had been. Although surrendering does result in some pretty immediate benefits, losing control can feel like a big drawback. I could tell by Rick's reaction that she was becoming more intimate with her husband, but I had a hard time convincing her that this was progress. Kim's new respect, however imperfect, helped Rick tap into his own

Prescription for alleviating panic

Has your husband done anything out of the ordinary lately? Regardless of whether you think it's something negative or positive, it's a good indication that your marriage is changing for the better as a result of your surrendering.

power and do what pleased him the most. He probably would not have done so had Kim not surrendered first.

Often the only validation we get for surrendering to our husbands (besides the pats on our back from other surrendered wives) is that our mates do things they never did before. For instance, one woman called to tell me her husband had called a travel agent. Another woman's shy husband ended up having a great time at a party because he walked up and introduced himself to strangers. My husband bought and started religiously using a day-planner. None of these actions constitutes a modern miracle for mankind, but each of them was a departure from what these husbands *normally* did. This unusual and attractive behavior is at least partly the result of feeling a new freedom.

Early in my surrendering, a close family friend came to stay with us. I asked him if he could see the difference in my behavior. "I can't see any difference in how you act," he told me, "but I can sure see the difference in John. He seems so much more alive."

I wasn't surrendering perfectly, but I knew my behavior had changed. Still, nobody was standing up to cheer me on. This was disappointing because I was making a Herculean effort to change and I wanted credit!

Again, the reason we don't get standing ovations for our new behavior is that it isn't extraordinary. It's certainly revolutionary compared to what we were doing before, but in the great scheme of things, we are only coming up to par. Just as no one stands up and applauds when you pay your bills on time or brush your teeth every day, no one will cheer because you are meeting the minimum requirement of being polite to your mate.

I THINK I'LL GO EAT SOME WORMS

Another difficulty you might encounter when you

first begin surrendering is what I call Worm Syndrome. Worm Syndrome happens when you first become aware that you are doing something you wish you weren't—but you can't stop doing it yet! I call it Worm Syndrome because it makes you feel so rotten about yourself, you're tempted to go out and eat some worms. If you're like me, you will also have a feeling of profound sadness when you compare your new behavior to your old habits. Once you begin surrendering even the tiniest little bit, you will begin to see the horror of your old self.

This happened to Margaret when she and her husband Glenn went to a restaurant that was partly self-service. On previous visits, Margaret's objections had won out over Glenn's desire to leave a tip. This time, when Margaret shrugged and didn't object to his idea, Glenn put some money on the table before they left. Suddenly she knew that each of the dozens of times they had been there before, Glenn had probably wanted to leave a tip, but didn't because of her disapproval. "Seeing with this new perspective, I feel awful about everything I did before," she told me.

I felt the same way when I watched my husband quit a job he had hated for four years and get a higher-paying one that he liked better shortly after I surrendered. I knew he had hesitated to leave his job because of my fear of financial insecurity. I realized I had been discouraging him from making a change because of *my* fear.

Sure, our husbands could have done things differently if they really wanted to, but they would have had to do it against the wishes of the one person in the world who matters most to them. So it's pretty sad to see how you've been keeping your best friend and lover from doing the big things or even the little things that would make him happy. Plus, if you can't stop controlling your husband perfectly

"Become a possibilitarian. No matter how dark things seem to be or actually are, raise your sights and see possibilities--always see them, for they're always there."

— Norman Vincent Peale

(and nobody can), every time you slip, you feel shame and self-judgment on top of your sadness.

As an analogy, let's say that a huge news story came out saying that drinking coffee causes hair loss. Upon hearing this news, you might decide to give up drinking coffee to preserve your hair, even though you're in the habit of having a cup or two every day.

The next day you get up and walk over to the coffee maker as usual and start a fresh pot. Then, just as you're about to take a sip, you remember you made an agreement with yourself to give it up for good. With the tempting aroma overtaking you and the comfort of a small sip just inches from your mouth, you decide to postpone your resolution for one more day. Now, as you continue to drink this cup, and have one or two more later on, you enjoy it just as you always have, but something is different. Each time you drink it, you feel a twinge of self-recrimination. "I'm making my hair fall out!" you moan to yourself. You tell yourself you really should stop and stop now, but you can't. At least not yet.

Now you're misery is complete, because not only can you not stop drinking coffee, you also can't enjoy it without feeling guilty now that you have this new information. You will have no peace until you either give up coffee, or invest in a wig and say to hell with your hair.

Surrendering is the same way. Knowing how to become more intimate with your husband does not necessarily give you the courage to do it immediately. There is that uncomfortable transition during which each time you are disrespectful, you recognize it and wince with self-recrimination. You wish you weren't doing this, but you're doing it, and this is where the worms come in.

Surrendering is difficult and takes tremendous courage. Nobody does it perfectly, or even very well at first.

"The average man is more interested in a woman who is interested in him than he is in a woman --any woman--with beautiful legs."

— *Marlene Dietrich*

Still, having the information and taking a stab at doing it *is* progress. At least now you know what to do differently. If your hair is falling out in clumps and you find out that coffee consumption is the reason, it's progress to at least see the connection between the two–even if you can't stop right away.

The problem is, knowing but not changing doesn't feel like progress. It feels like torture because every time you're disrespectful or critical or demeaning or dismissing, a huge billboard lights up in your brain and says, "See!?! You're doing it again!!!" Some of us also inwardly scream insults at ourselves like:

"Why would anyone want to be married to you!"

"You are a terrible wife!"

"You are absolute hell to live with!"

No matter how poorly you're doing, there is no need to insult yourself, even if it's just in your head. A lot of things get started in your head, so what you tell yourself about yourself is actually pretty important. When you notice that you're insulting yourself in your head, apologize to yourself immediately. You might say something like: "I'm sorry I said that to you. I didn't mean it. You have lots of good qualities too, like a terrific sense of humor (or whatever is true for you). You're making progress with surrendering, so good job!"

Say this out loud, to give it more importance than the insults in your head. This will probably feel entirely silly, but then again some people will think this whole concept of surrendering is ridiculous. So as long as you're going to be silly, you might as well be nice to yourself while you're doing it.

When I tell some women to apologize to themselves, they try to explain that they *really* are not doing a good job. They tell me they've taken one step forward but

"Without change, something sleeps inside us and seldom awakens. The sleeper must awaken."

— *Frank Herberr*

ten steps back. They tell me how completely rotten and horrible they've been.

If you have apologized to your husband for being disrespectful even once, withheld criticism even once, deferred to his thinking even once, let him solve his own problem even once, or expressed your gratitude for him even once, you have begun to surrender. Even if you raged at him and berated him and dismissed him ten times after that, you have begun to surrender. Give yourself credit for what you have done right. Acknowledge to yourself that you have taken action towards changing your life, and encourage yourself to try again tomorrow.

"The best cure for anger

is delay."

— Seneca, A.D. 63

If you continue to do this, tomorrow will be different. You will not be perfect, but you will progress. Instead of clobbering yourself mentally each time you say something regrettable, give yourself credit for having this new insight. After all, before you read this book, you probably didn't even realize you had some disrespectful habits. At least you know that now!

Even if you have done nothing else, you have made progress by getting this book, reading it, and being aware of times that you wish you hadn't said what you said. Give yourself a pat on the back, and keep reading.

THE TRUTH ABOUT TELLING THE TRUTH

When leaders of the nations of the world get together, you never hear one of them saying to the other, "Your breath smells like something crawled up there and died!" This is probably not because premiers and kings and prime ministers never have bad breath. Rather, it's because our leaders are trained in diplomacy. They even learn to have good manners in the culture they are visiting. For instance, when the president of the United States goes to Japan, he bows, even though it's not customary at home.

While the rest of us were commenting on the shape and size of Gorbachev's birthmark, the president was engaged in diplomatic conversations where it never came up.

Just imagine the problems that would arise if our leaders did not use diplomacy. We'd probably have to go to war with countries that were angry with us for insulting their leaders' breath. Then there'd be wounded soldiers and orphaned children just because some diplomat didn't have the sense to put duct tape over his mouth.

Fortunately, you don't see this much because as a nation, we are willing to go to great lengths to keep relations friendly with other countries. For some reason, it's much harder to extend our husbands the same courtesy. I often hear women justifying their lack of diplomacy by saying, "But it's the truth! He DID pick terrible stocks to invest in! He DID pick his teeth at the governor's ball!" The truth is, it's not always such a great idea to tell your husband the truth.

I'm *not* suggesting that you should lie to him–just that not every truth is worth saying out loud. You may be absolutely right when you say that it's his own fault that he bounced a check, but what good does it do to say that? Four-year-olds often tell the truth because they have not yet learned that part of being civilized is refraining from commenting about fat people, women with mustaches, and speech impediments. Your husband deserves the same diplomacy and grace that you would offer to any stranger next to you in a waiting room.

Sure it feels good to be right. Everyone likes to feel smart, and saying "I told you so" is undeniably satisfying. In my experience, this kind of satisfaction is not worth the price of admission because it puts distance between my partner and me. If you would rather snuggle and giggle in bed together than stay up late arguing, don't tell him these

Reporter: What do you think of Western civilization?

Gandhi: I think it's a great idea.

kinds of truths.

Taking this idea one step further, I also suggest that you remember to do things that are polite in other cultures–in this case, the male culture. For instance, talking about feelings among other women is fine, but not so with men. Asking a man how he feels is about like asking a woman about her weight. At best, it's uncomfortable, and at worst, it's embarrassing. It's not that hard to learn a few customs–like bowing in Japan–to use as social grease in your marriage.

So if you don't tell unpleasant truths or ask your husband how he feels, how in the world are you going to have an intimate conversation with him? Try listening! One woman complained that her husband would follow her around the house when she was trying to do things. Then it occurred to her that he was trying to talk to her. Another noticed that she interrupted her husband every few minutes by jumping up to get the laundry, talking to her toddler, or answering the phone. Still another wife caught herself asking her husband questions, then tuning him out as soon as he began to answer.

As an experiment, I went out to dinner with my husband and tried just listening—not talking about myself—for the whole meal. It wasn't easy. He had plenty of interesting things to say, but I kept getting distracted by my own thoughts and thinking of things I wanted to tell him. I had to make a conscious effort to keep listening. I wondered if he would ask me why I was so quiet, but he didn't. He probably didn't want to ruin his one chance of getting some airtime.

The key to having intimate conversations with your husband is to make yourself available to listen to what he says. Encourage him by making eye contact, staying quiet, and asking questions whenever appropriate. Tilt your head

Prescription for restoring civility

Write about three occasions when you told your husband a hurtful truth. What resulted from this? What was your motivation? Was there any benefit for you? Was it really necessary?

a little to the side to indicate your interest in what he's saying. Raise your eyebrows and say, "oh?" to encourage him to say more. He may not tell you his feelings, but your husband will tell you about what's important to him, what's going on in his life, and what his interests are. Knowing those things is what makes your relationship intimate.

CRITICAL MASS

In physics, when something reaches critical mass, it has reached the point right before something is going to change dramatically or else explode. Critical mass is also the term I use to describe what happens after you've begun surrendering and the central issue of your entire marriage is called into focus. For some it could last only a few minutes, for others it could last for weeks. You will know when you're in it because the pressure to pick up your old controlling behavior will feel immense. You will think to yourself, "Ah-ha! This is the crux of what has always been a problem for us, and it's about to change." A dramatic, positive change will take place if you don't respond in your old way. This is similar to resisting bait but even more significant.

One of the symptoms of critical mass is feeling like you absolutely can't live like this anymore. Your husband may seem like he's in a funk—either cranky and unhappy all the time, or distant and distracted. Here's what's going on when that happens: As a result of taking steps to surrender to your husband, you are making significant spiritual changes. If your husband is going to keep up with you, he too will have to grow dramatically. As an analogy, imagine the two of you are learning to speak French. You spend ten hours the first week listening to tapes and reading a book, and by the end of the week you've got a few phrases down. Your husband hasn't put as much time in, so when you try

"Politeness is the art of selecting among one's real thoughts."

— Madame de Stael

"All life is an experiment."

— *Ralph Waldo Emerson*

to practice what you've learned with him, he stares at you blankly because he doesn't understand. He might even get frustrated and angry with you for trying to speak to him in a language he doesn't understand. One way to get around this situation is to revert back to your original language. Another solution is to simply continue to speak to him in French and wait for him to catch on. The problem with taking the first option is that you end up right back where you were—in a marriage that is lonely and doesn't meet your needs. The problem with the second version is that it requires incredible patience and faith.

Unfortunately for me, I'm not a very patient person, so when my husband was in a funk not too long ago, I confronted him about it. I said, "What's the matter with you? If you're not reading the paper, you're watching television, listening to the radio, or taking a nap!" Then I tacked on an "I miss you" at the end because just then I remembered that I'm trying to be a surrendered wife. When I finished, he stared at me blankly, shrugged his shoulders, and said he was too tired to talk about it. I might as well have been mooing like a cow for all the good it did me.

Luckily, I discussed this issue with a friend who reminded me that I needed to tend to my own self-care and give him the space to solve his own problems. Sure enough, as soon as I did what she suggested, I noticed my husband seemed more available. Once he got in the hang of the latest changes in our relationship, everything was fine.

One of the big fears I had about making these changes to begin with was that I would upset the balance in my marriage too much and end up alone. I found that the other surrendered wives shared a similar notion. We erroneously believed that if we grew too much, our husbands would not be able to keep up. We were motivated to stay stuck where we were, even if it wasn't very comfortable, because we were afraid we'd lose our marriages if we didn't.

I'm pleased to report that our experience has been the exact opposite. No matter how quickly we take action and no matter how dramatic, as long as we are growing along spiritual lines our husbands always seem to keep pace with us. For instance, my husband is now handling the finances for us; I recently asked him if I could take them back just to see what he would say. At first he laughed, but when I persisted and acted as though I was serious, his answer was a firm "hell, no!" Clearly, that change has taken root.

When you are in critical mass, you may feel lonely. You'll probably miss your husband and wax nostalgic for the good old days. Remind yourself that if the good old days had really been that good, you wouldn't have bought or borrowed this book and read it. Stay on course and the rewards will be great. If you fear that your marriage is dying, you're probably right. A better, stronger connection will bloom in its place.

I became aware of this rebirth process in my own marriage about a year ago while my husband and I were out to breakfast. I was just relaxing and letting him open doors for me. In the crowded waiting area, my shy husband approached a couple and asked permission to take an empty chair. He pulled the chair up and nodded at me to sit down, so I did. Then he asked me if I wanted some juice. I nodded, so he filled a glass and brought it to me. It was a small moment, but we were both conscious of a shift that day. I was acknowledging my willingness to receive, and he was responding with a willingness to take care of me. I felt the power in our yin and yangness. I knew that we could never go back to the old way.

That is why, for our ninth anniversary I decided to take a big plunge by taking his last name. In our old marriage, I had kept my maiden name as a symbol of my identity as a feminist. Perhaps on some level, I was also reluc-

"If you are patient in one moment of anger, you will escape a hundred days of sorrow."

— *Chinese Proverb*

tant and terrified to merge with my husband. In our new marriage, I wanted to do something that symbolized my profound respect for him and acknowledge the intimacy we shared.

"What a new face courage puts on everything!"

— *Ralph Waldo Emerson*

Ironically, since I started respecting my husband, he seems so much more worthy of my respect. While I don't do this surrendering thing perfectly, I now enjoy being married to my wonderful, handsome, capable husband. Today, I have the intimate marriage I always dreamed was possible. If you surrender to your husband, you will too.

Really.

Surrendered Circles

The very first Surrendered Circle met on a Thursday afternoon in November of 1998. I invited some friends to come over for a pot-luck and to form a community of women who would support each other in surrendering to their husbands. I felt lucky to have four other women who were willing to meet once a month for this purpose. As word spread, the meetings grew. I wanted to keep the meeting in my living room, so when the group reached a dozen, I started a waiting list and began offering workshops.

I hardly know where to begin to explain the importance of the Surrendered Circle for my journey and those of the women I know. We laughed and cried and ate together, and somehow found safety, healing, and miracles with each other's help. From the very first meeting, we felt a tremendous bond. No matter how discouraged and hopeless we felt before we got there, we left feeling energized, hopeful, and strong. We called each other frequently during the month to get extra support and advice.

Through this experience, we realized that mutual support was a key ingredient to successful surrendering. Surrendering was no easy process, but something about doing it together made it easier. None of us could do this thing alone. Every woman who attempts to surrender to her husband needs this kind of support. If you cannot find a Surrendered Circle to join in your area, then I urge you to form a group yourself. This chapter contains explicit instructions on how to start your own Surrendered Circle. Meeting once a month with even just one other wife will help you find the courage to continue on this path.

At each of the meetings, one of the women in the group read her Surrendered Wife story. This was a written account of her path up until this point as it related to surrendering. She told us about what she learned from watching her parents' marriage, her relationship with her father, her patterns in dating and relationships, ways that she tried to control her husband, and things that had happened to her that could have caused her to feel terror. Most importantly, the stories also included the miracles she had experienced since starting to surrender.

There is no right or wrong way to write your Surrendered Wife story. Some are long, some are not. Some are chronological, others are not. In our circle, most of us cried reading our stories out loud. Those of us who were listening were honored to witness this tenderness and enjoyed a tremendous connection with the storyteller.

The most important thing to remember when you are writing your story is to be honest. Take risks, and show more of yourself than you are comfortable revealing. Tell about things that are embarrassing or shameful to you. Use this as an opportunity to let the others in the group really get to know you. This is good practice for being intimate with your husband. As you share your story with someone else, you are practicing vulnerability, which is precisely what you'll need in your marriage.

Of course, if you are going to expose yourself this way, safety has to be a top priority in the circle. Therefore, part of being a member of the circle is making a commitment to hold what you hear in safe hands. The Surrendered Circle is a sacred gathering. Do not treat it as anything less.

"All of us at certain moments of our lives need to take advice and to receive help from other people."

— Alexis Carrell

Criticism and gossip have no place among the members of the Surrendered Circle. Only positive feedback is appropriate.

Our Surrendered Circle meets only once a month, but you could certainly meet more frequently if you wanted. Any gathering place is fine, as long as it is private so that everyone can share freely. A living room works great. You can also use the exercises throughout this book as group exercises for your circle. I've included three examples of exercises we did as a group. You can also come up with your own if you like.

Following is the format we used for our monthly meetings, which started at 12:30 with visiting and settling in. Feel free to modify it to suit your purposes.

"Fear less, hope more;

Whine less, breathe more;

Talk less, say more;

Hate less, love more;

And all good things are

yours."

— Swedish Proverb

FORMAT FOR A SURRENDERED CIRCLE
12:45p.m.
Hello and welcome to the Surrendered Circle. Would you join me in saying the serenity prayer?
God, grant me the serenity to accept the things I cannot change, the courage to change the things I can, and the wisdom to know the difference.

Introduction
Welcome to the Surrendered Circle, a community of women who gather to support each other in surrendering to their husbands. Please help yourself to some lunch, and make yourself comfortable. We will begin with brief introductions around the room. If you wish, you may share with us your name, how long you've been married, the ages of your children, and how long you've been practicing the principles of a surrendered wife. I'll start....

Pass the Ask-it Basket

This is the Q&A basket. If you have a question you would like addressed in the meeting, please write it down and we'll read it out loud later on. You may sign your name or remain anonymous.

I've asked someone to read out loud:
- How We Knew We Needed to Surrender
- What We Did to Surrender
- What Happened When We Surrendered

Now it is time for the leader to read her Surrendered Wife story. **Leader reads story until 1:20 or 1:25 p.m.**

Ask the leader if she would like feedback

Starting on the leader's right, we'll go around the circle and briefly give the leader positive feedback on her story, such as what you could relate to, what touched you, or why you are grateful to hear it.

Group Exercise

Time for group exercise or discussion of completed exercise until 2:05 p.m.

Q&A from the Ask-it Basket until 2:20 (or group discussion) That's all the time we have, but I'd like to make a few announcements before we close. The next Surrendered Circle will be held here on _____ at 12:30. Please bring food or drinks to share. You can take numbers from the phone list to call other surrendered wives between meetings if you wish. Are there any other announcements?

Close at 2:25p.m. with serenity prayer

HOW WE KNEW WE NEEDED TO SURRENDER

BY CHRISTINE GORDON

We, who have chosen the path of the surrendered wife, gather together in love, support, and friendship. Our path is a sacred one, and so we close our circle to gossip and criticism, keeping our hearts and minds open to one another. We open ourselves to health - physical, emotional, and spiritual.

The circle is an ancient symbol of marriage. The wedding ring itself reminds us of a commitment to a life never-ending. The circle marks a sacred boundary around a man and a woman who together form a new family. We are conscious of a society that has lost its footing on the marriage path. With God as our guide, we have discovered that surrendering in our marriages gives us a new freedom we had not known before.

For a wife to surrender means she is willing to release her grip on her husband's life, thereby making his own journey possible. We have found that marriage works best when we let our husbands be the men and fathers only they know how to be. Surrendering is a process of celebrating our femaleness— our God-given right to receive life's blessings of love, companionship, prosperity, and family life. We can fulfill our womanhood only when we give our husbands the freedom to stand tall in their manhood. In extricating our grip, we find we have renewed energy for life's many joys.

Here are some of the signs that told us it was time to surrender:

- Feelings of superiority to our husbands.
- A long-harbored suspicion that we had married beneath ourselves.

- "Henpecking" or disrespecting our husbands behind their backs—particularly in the company of other wives.
- Encouraging other wives to disrespect their husbands.
- Disrespecting our husbands publicly and privately.
- Often hearing ourselves say the words, "I told my husband..."
- Believing everything would be okay if our husbands would just do as we said.
- Compulsively looking for the worst in our husbands.
- Eavesdropping on our husband's conversations to ensure everything was handled correctly.
- Feeling that there was only one adult in the family–us!
- Feelings of being overburdened in parenting our children.
- Increasing fear around family decisions.
- Doing for our husbands what they were capable of doing for themselves.
- Recurring anxiety and depression.
- Physical exhaustion, often including chronic illness.
- A loss of interest in sex by either partner.
- Increasing resentment and jealousy at their victories in life.
- Rejecting their gifts until they could no longer risk giving.
- Often fantasizing about divorce or life with a man who would better match us.
- Discounting the reasons we had chosen our husband in the first place.
- Feeling that our needs had gone unmet for so long that we lost hope.
- Inability to trust our husbands in even the smallest matter.
- Finding our obsession to control had become so loud

that we could no longer hear the voice of God.

WHAT WE DID TO SURRENDER TO OUR HUSBANDS

Taking the following actions resulted in miraculous changes in our marriages. Please note that we do not recommend them to women who are in physically abusive relationships, or whose husbands have an active addiction, such as alcoholism.

We have also found that telling our husbands about these practices, while very tempting, is counter-productive. Announcing to our husbands that we would now be trying to respect them was no improvement at all. We talked to other wives freely, but we found it was not in our best interest to talk about the practices of a surrendered wife with our husbands. Instead, we urge you to simply take these actions as best you can.

Here are the things that we did, to the best of our ability, to surrender to our husbands:

1. We practiced graciously and gratefully receiving from our husbands whenever possible.
2. We released our inappropriate expectations for our husbands and focused on appreciating their gifts.
3. We refrained from asking our husbands to do things *we* wanted them to do.
4. We concentrated on taking care of ourselves first, knowing that our own contentment was the key to a happy household.
5. We relinquished control of the household finances and relied on our husbands to give us what we need.
6. We apologized for being disrespectful whenever we contradicted, criticized, or dismissed our husbands' thoughts and ideas.
7. We made ourselves sexually available to our husbands.

8. We deferred to our husbands' thinking when we had conflicting opinions.

9. We told our husbands what we wanted in the way of clothing, household items, babies, vacations, etc., and allowed them to provide those things for us.

10. We followed their direction and leadership, except when to do so would injure us physically or spiritually.

11. We discussed our problems with other married women to gain perspective, and so that we didn't have to rely on our husbands as our only emotional support.

12. We refrained from offering our husbands advice or teaching them how to do things.

13. We acknowledged our hurt feeling by saying "ouch," our loneliness by saying "I miss you," and our gratitude by saying "thank you."

14. We listened to our husbands' problems without offering solutions for them, even when it meant we had to watch them suffer indefinitely.

WHAT HAPPENED WHEN WE SURRENDERED

BY LYNNAE BENNETT

The miracles in our lives are countless today. The commitment, dedication and the partnership in our marriages is what many of our hearts have yearned so deeply for. Many of us have dreamt of this type of relationship and today we are living it. One day at a time, we respect our husbands. We respect their choices, their decisions, and their dreams. In return, we are given the opportunity to receive love, help, guidance, and financial abundance. By surrendering and releasing control we give back to our husbands their own space and we are given back our own individual energy to create what we want.

For many of us, this is not an easy task. At many

times it almost feels impossible. But with the support and experience of other surrendered wives, we walk through it together. When we become willing to try the suggestions, the results amaze us.

When we begin changing our behaviors towards our husbands, which for most of us is centered from fear, control, anger, resentment, jealousy, and ego, we no longer need to worry about everything. We no longer need to do everything, plan everything, manipulate and control everything.

We released and let go of the grip and believe and trust in the God of our hearts.

EXERCISES

I. What we learned from our Mothers
When everyone in the group has completed this exercise, we will go around the circle and share the answers out loud.

1. My mother thought my father's parenting was

_____.

2. My mother thought the way my father handled money

was _____.

3. My mother thought the way my father dressed was

_____.

4. My mother's attitude towards my dad was mostly

_____.

5. My mother's attitude towards my husband is

_____.

6. The person who made most of the decisions at home was

_____.

7. My impression of my mother is that she is/was a

_____ woman.

8. When my mother is worried, she shows it by

_____.

9. My mother thought my father's job was _____.

10. The person who controlled the money at our house was

_____.

11. My parents' marriage was/is _____.

12. What I learned from my mother about marriage is _____

_____

_____

13. What I wish my mother knew about my marriage is_____

_____

_____

14. How am I like my mother in my marriage? _____

_____

_____

_____

15. How am I different from her in my marriage?_____

_____

_____

_____

16. In the future, I want to change how I behave in my mar-

riage by _____

II. Receiving

Today's exercise is about learning to receive and take credit
for our gifts. Take a minute to think of and write down a
sincere compliment for the woman on your left.

We are going to go around the circle and each of you will have a chance to look the woman to your left in the eyes and give her a compliment. Your job when you are receiving the compliment is to meet her gaze and do your best to let it all in. I suggest you respond by saying, "thank you, that's true." Or, if you can't do that, at least say "thank you." DO NOT say anything to discount the compliment. If you need duct tape to put around your mouth, we have some available. Do your very best to receive the compliment graciously. Who would like to start?

"Our doubts are traitors and make us lose the good we oft might win by fearing to attempt."

— William Shakespeare

Now I want you to take just a minute to think about your best physical feature and write that down. We are going to go around the circle and tell the women on our right what our best feature is. Do not whisper this, or put in modifiers such as "kind of" or "pretty good." Rather, I would prefer that you use words like gorgeous, outstanding, fabulous and amazing, as in "I have a gorgeous face." Who would like to start?

III. Gratitude

You have exactly five minutes to write a gratitude list about your man. When you are through, you can read it to the group if you choose. (*Set a kitchen timer for five minutes.*) Ready? Go!

Who would like to read theirs out loud? (Go around the circle and read lists.)

This exercise can be turned into a present for your husband. Get a small journal or notebook with blank pages and write one thing from the list on each of the pages. Use colored pens or crayons to decorate the pages.

THE ELECTRONIC COMMUNITY OF SURRENDERED WIVES

If you are in an isolated area and find it impossible to meet with other women even once a month, then one alternative resource for support is the Internet. As of this writing, I host a website at http://www.surrenderedwife.com where women post on an electronic bulletin board about their challenges and successes in the journey of surrendering to their husbands. I also hope to make this a resource for Surrendered Circles to announce their contact information. If nothing else, you can gather e-mail addresses and ask for advice there. This will help sustain you somewhat, and connect you to women throughout the world who are on this same path. However difficult your journey, you are not alone. There are many of us who are learning to relinquish inappropriate control and traveling towards true intimacy with our husbands. I welcome your comments, questions, wisdom and support.

"Our thoughts, our words, and deeds are the threads of the net which we throw around ourselves."

— *Swami Vivekananda*

Give the Gift of an Intimate Marriage to Your Friends and Family

To order *The Surrendered Wife*, complete and mail the form below:

YES, I want _____ copies of *The Surrendered Wife: A Woman's Spiritual Guide to True Intimacy with a Man* at $12.95 each, plus $3.95 shipping per book (California residents please add $1 sales tax per book). Canadian orders must be accompanied by a postal money order in U.S. funds. Allow 15 days for delivery.

I've enclosed a check or money order for $_____
or
Please charge my ❑ Visa ❑ MasterCard ❑ Discover
❑ American Express

Name_____

Organization_____

Address_____

City/State/Zip_____

Phone_____ E-mail_____

Card #_____ Exp. Date_____

Signature_____

Mail this form with checks made payable to:
St. Monday Publishing
3051 Hayes Ave.
Costa Mesa, CA 92626